99

Problems

— but a —

Baby

Ain't One

2/5/15

Melissa—
From one brutal
bitch to another!
You have a good friend
who I love. All the
best sister!

♡,
Megyn

99 Problems but a Baby Ain't One

A Memoir about
Cancer, Adoption, and
My Love for Jay-Z

Megan Silianoff

99 Problems but a Baby Ain't One
A Memoir about Cancer, Adoption, and My Love for Jay-Z

Brown Books Small Press
16250 Knoll Trail Drive, Suite 205
Dallas, Texas 75248
www.BBSmallPress.com
(972) 381-0009

A New Era in Publishing™

ISBN 978-1-61254-137-2
LCCN 2013942941

Printed in the United States
10 9 8 7 6 5 4 3 2 1

For more information or to contact the author, please go to
www.GreetingsFromTX.com

To Danny

Fear not when, fear not why
Fear not much while we're alive
Life is for livin' not livin' uptight
'Til you somewhere up in the sky

—Jay-Z, Young Forever

CONTENTS

Part Two

Part Three

FREQUENTLY ASKED QUESTIONS

Is this a blog? Or a book? I'm confused.

Great question. It's both. It's a book written in blog style. Sound complicated? It's not. But tell your friends that it is—you'll sound smart. Just don't brag. Nobody likes a person who's super uppity about the books they read.

Is this about cancer and adoption though? I'm not sure I want to read about either of those topics. They seem a bit heavy, you know?

I don't blame you. Cancer—*ugh*! Adoption—*meh*! Total downers. I assure you, however, this is not a depressing story. It's actually very uplifting. You know how you feel right after watching *The Blind Side*? Or *Remember The Titans*? It's like that.

Really? I'm still not sure. Can I have my money back if I disagree?

Uh, I'm not sure how that works.

I've flipped through this book and noticed you mention Rachel Bilson several times. What's the deal? Do you know her or something?

Rachel Bilson is my style icon. That may have come up once or twice.

So this is all true? Everything you wrote about really happened?

One hundred percent. I took some creative liberties with the timeline, just so the story would make sense to you readers who don't know me personally. I also changed the names of a few characters, such as my baby's birthparents, our adoption caseworker, and some (not all) of my friends. "Ann," for example, with whom I reference smoking pot on page 42, is not really "Ann." I changed her name because she has a really legit, serious job now.

I changed all my doctors' names in this story because I'm not sure about the rules when it comes to doctors, confidentiality, getting sued, and all that stuff. I prefer not to be sued with regard to this book and just life in general. Also, sometimes the "blog comments" that appear at the end of entries are things that my friends and family said to me in real life. I included them in this story in the form of comments.

Is this, like, chick lit? It seems pretty girly.

Not necessarily. I like to think there is a little something in here for everybody. I reference "basketball" on page 41 and "football" on page 129.

Is this book funny? It seems like it's supposed to be funny, but I just can't be sure.

I think it's funny, but obviously I'm partial. What's "funny" is so subjective. For example, tons of people thought Pee Wee Herman was funny. I was never one of them. I actually thought he was quite creepy. Especially when he was arrested for indecent exposure years later.

Fine, I'll read your book. I just hope it doesn't suck.

Me too, reader!

PROLOGUE

Megan Silianoff, twenty-eight, is a healthy young woman consistently mistaken for Rachel Bilson. (She wishes.) Megan resides in Chicago, Illinois, and is married to Danny Silianoff, thirty-five, consistently mistaken for Kevin James. (Despite his wishes.)

The two met when Megan was working as a recruiter at a staffing firm. Megan's firm was hired to find employees for the software company of which Danny was vice president. Megan was not overly successful at finding employees, but she was excellent at flirting with Danny. Despite her poor professional showing, Megan's flirting was enough to lock down the account and, months later, a husband.

Megan and Danny have a dog named Booker, whom they adopted from the Anti-Cruelty Society. Booker is a Vizsla/Beagle mix, though his most distinctive characteristic is his raging separation anxiety.

Megan graduated from Augustana College in Rock Island, Illinois. She majored in speech communication and Spanish. Ironically, today Megan speaks little to no Spanish despite what it says on her résumé. Danny attended Northwood University in Dallas, Texas, on a golf scholarship.

Megan's interests include Urban Outfitters, *To Catch a Predator* with Chris Hanson, texting, shellac manicures, Chanel, Jay-Z, and long walks on the beach. Danny likes to golf.

Politically speaking, Megan is *pro* world peace and *anti* tanning tax. She thinks that Obama is sexy. Danny is conservative.

part one

Monday, September 6, 2010
I HAVE CANCER

Hi. I'm Megan. This is my blog. As you now know, I have cancer. If you're shocked, take comfort in knowing that I am too. This all started about a week ago. Actually, the doctors say I've likely had cancer for two years now. But I've only been in on it since Wednesday.

This blog is an attempt at damage control. While this is not a scandal, nor am I a celebrity, I want people to hear this from me. Also, I strongly dislike the way my mom tells people the news. I've overheard a few of her phone conversations, and they're just so depressing. I'd like to keep it a bit lighter, perhaps with a joke here and there.

News of my cancer diagnosis appears to be spreading like wildfire. I can't keep up with the e-mails I'm receiving. So this is my little PR blog. I'll let you know what's happening and when as things go down. So let's get you caught up until now.

Wednesday I had what was supposed to be a straightforward surgery to remove a small cyst on my ovary. Originally it was just supposed to be laparoscopic. My doc would go in with a little tube, get the cyst, and we'd both move on with our lives. Two days before the surgery I had my "pre-op" appointment. My doctor took one last ultrasound only to find the cyst had grown too large to do the procedure laparoscopically. She'd have to cut me open. I wasn't thrilled.

Despite it being more than I'd bargained for, the surgery was still supposed to be relatively simple and straightforward. I told everyone at work that I'd be back on Monday. Danny kissed me good-bye, and my doctor wheeled me back to the operating room. I was scared, but not scared enough given what was about to go down.

Midsurgery it was discovered that my ovary didn't have a cyst but rather "borderline tumors." Borderline tumors are cancerous. WTF. The doctors eased me into this information upon my regaining consciousness. At first it was the tumors "might" be cancerous. Then it was introducing me to an oncologist. A fucking oncologist! (My mom doesn't swear when she tells people. Another valid reason for this blog.)

I spent the next few days in the hospital. I eventually proved to the nurses and doctor that I was ready to go home. I could walk. I could eat. I could say, "I want to go home now." I was ready for release, but my test results weren't. We still hadn't received all of the pathology on what, specifically, was going on with my ovary. I left after making a plan with the oncologist that she'd call upon receiving my results. (It wasn't that an extensive of a plan.)

While all this was going down, my parents were in Wyoming on a vacation they'd been planning for over a year. They were doing Mount Rushmore, Yellowstone, Salt Lake City, and that whole scene. Even though I told them not to, they decided to fly home early to be with me. I felt bad. My dad had apparently seen a lot of wild buffalo in Jackson Hole, Wyoming, and I could tell he was pretty jacked about it.

Friday night I had just sat down to dinner with Danny and my mom. We had ordered in Indian, my fave, from India House in River North. My phone rang. My stomach dropped at the sound of my ringer. It was 8:00 at night, but I just knew it was my doctor. I answered the phone. It was not good news. Not even borderline. (Pun intended. Are puns jokes?) The cancer had spread into my abdominal cavity and I'd need chemo. I felt nauseous and faint and remember crouching down to the ground. I didn't cry, but I was crippled with horror. For the first time in my life, I didn't clear my plate of Palak Paneer.

Danny and my mom could tell it wasn't good news, and the doctor could tell that they were in the background. She told me to put her on speakerphone. She must have been used to this sort of thing. The doctor and my mom carried the rest of the conversation. I can't tell you much about what they said or how I felt because I had blacked out in terror. All I knew was that the doc said I would need chemo and the cancer had spread into my abdomen. I had an appointment for Friday morning to learn more.

That night was hell. I was in shock. I also was gravely concerned about Danny and my mom. Poor Danny didn't sign up for this. He had just gone through this with his dad a few years ago, and his dad didn't make it. And my mom. My poor mom.

I had forty-eight hours until my appointment with the oncologist. I spent forty of them obsessing about losing my hair. The other eight were spent watching my new favorite show, *The Rachel Zoe Project*. The irony of Rachel's famous phrase "I die" was not lost on me. Her interest in her husband Rodger, however, was. Rodger is sort of a tool, no? (Jokes!)

At last, the time came for us to meet with the oncologist. Danny, my mom, and I waited in the examination room. My doctor entered. I wanted her to peel off the Band-Aid quickly. Just say what she had to say and get on with it. Unfortunately, that wasn't her style. She wanted to tread very slowly, asking me if I was okay or how I was doing after every tiny piece of information she delivered.

"How are you doing, Megan? I know this must be difficult. Are you doing okay?"

"I know this is unexpected. How are you holding up, Megan? Are you okay?"

"I did receive the results of your pathology, Megan, and I'd like to review them with you now. Is that okay?"

JESUS CHRIST, LADY! JUST GET ON WITH IT! (I didn't tell her that, but I did mouth it to Danny when she wasn't looking.)

Like so many times in life, we received both good news and bad news.

Bad News:

While performing a very quick exam, the doctor found a cyst in my boob. While this is not good, she feels it's most likely just a coincidence and not related to the ovarian cancer. To be sure, she's scheduling a mammogram for me next week.

Good News:

The particular type of chemo I need for the ovarian cancer will not make me lose my hair. I think that warrants repeating. I'M NOT LOSING MY HAIR!

This is, of course, assuming the cancer hasn't spread outside my abdomen—I'll have a CAT scan this week to make sure. But initially, good news.

This has been a lot of information. Information overload perhaps. Are you guys overwhelmed? I am. If you made it to this point, you're up to speed. You know as much as I do. Heavy, huh? That's why jokes are crucial. You guys got any?

To sum up:

1. I have ovarian cancer.
2. Hopefully it hasn't spread.
3. I have a cyst in my boob. Hopefully it's not cancer.
4. I need chemo. It won't make me lose my hair.
5. Overall, WTF.

4 COMMENTS

Janelle:

I can't believe this is happening to you. Please let me know if there is anything I can do other than providing you with this awesome joke.

Question: How do you know when you're really drunk?
Answer: You get into a taxicab and think the fare is the time.

Megan replied:

Ha! That's not a joke. You probably just did that this weekend.

Marc:

Megan, finally figured out how to comment on this blog! Trying to do it from a Blackberry is like hacking into the Matrix! We love you and are thinking about you.

Justin:

Megan, you've had more views on this blog in one week than I've had on mine in three years. That's not a joke.

Thursday, September 9, 2010
GOOD NEWS

It's good news! The CAT scan showed that the cancer has not spread outside my abdominal region! I'm pumped! Based on this, my doctor is hopeful about the imminent ultrasound of my boob. I'm not celebrating until I know for sure. I am, however, using a lot of exclamation points!!!!

If my mammogram on Thursday goes equally well, I'm out of the woods, relatively speaking. "Out of the woods" meaning not losing my hair, my biggest concern at this point. Assuming the boob cyst is benign, I'll simply have a hysterectomy and undergo chemo. Two weeks ago, I wouldn't have used the word "simply" in that sentence. However, if this is the case, my cancer won't be life threatening or hair threatening, and that's all I'm asking for at this point.

Thanks to everyone for your prayers and well-wishes. The amount of people who have reached out is overwhelming. Maybe I'm a celebrity after all?

1 COMMENT

Adam:

Megan, I kind of feel like I'm writing in a yearbook. You know, on a page that everyone is going to see and read? Makes me nervous. Anyway, until you've kicked this cancer you'll continue to play a critical role in my daughter's bedtime routine:

- Brush teeth
- Read Elmo book
- Pray for Megan

Have a great summer. Stay sweet. Can't wait until we're seniors next year!

Saturday, September 11, 2010
GIVING THANKS

Today didn't go as I would have hoped. The cyst in my breast looks like cancer. The radiologist, who was a bit young and pretty for my liking, said she's about 80 percent sure. I prefer my doctors old and academic looking. A thick accent is also comforting. I go tomorrow for a biopsy and will receive the official verdict Monday—but it's not looking good.

The gene that causes ovarian cancer can be the same gene that causes breast cancer. So it's not that the cancer spread, but their existence may be related. That's how I understand it anyway. I've yet to talk to my oncologist. But based on the brief conversation with the radiologist, this is a game changer. I assume I'll need the breast cancer chemo, and that's the chemo that makes your hair fall out. I'll also need a double mastectomy with breast reconstruction.

There's not much to say. It's definitely disappointing. I'm a fan of both my hair and my boobs so I'll be sorry to see them go. But there is no choice in this deal. The only choice is to deal with it and focus on the positive, and that's what I'm doing. Hence the following list. I'm making it for myself more than anyone else, but I'll share.

POSITIVE THINGS IN MY LIFE AND THIS SITUATION IN GENERAL

1. Danny Silianoff

I love my husband so much and couldn't ask for a better person to do this thing with. We share the same outlook and ambition in terms of adversity, and together I don't think there is much we can't accomplish.

2. My Immediate Family

I love my mom, dad, and brother. These people also happen to be my colleagues as I work in the family business. I'm thinking I can leverage a raise out this situation.

3. Booker

I love my dog.

4. Medicinal Marijuana

I've never, ever smoked pot. (Jokes!) But it can't hurt to look into this alternative medicine. I'll do whatever takes to feel better. I'll go that extra mile. If that happens to be a gravity bong, so be it.

5. Weight Loss

I'm down at least five pounds since this whole saga started. This could be just the jump start I need for a lucrative modeling career.

6. Friends

I'm lucky to have so many. If I need anything, I feel like I have a million people I could call.

7. *Friends*

The television show. That Chandler Bing cracks me up. "Pants. Like shorts. But longer!"—Chandler Bing.

8. Urban Outfitters

Bohemian chic at an affordable price point. I love you, Urban Outfitters!

9. India House: The Best Indian Restaurant in All of Chicago

This one pairs nicely with number 4 on this list. Number 5, however, not so much.

I think that's sufficient for now. Perhaps I'll continue later as it was very therapeutic. Thanks to everyone for your prayers and thoughts. Don't worry about me. If this has to happen to someone, I'm a good candidate. I'm healthy-ish, mentally strong, and don't take anything too seriously. I got this.

3 COMMENTS

Erin:

Megs, when this is all over, come visit Ryan and me in Denver. There are more marijuana shops than Starbucks. You know what competition does for price. They will be amazed that someone who has a legit reason (i.e., something more serious than swimmer's ear) is shopping with them.

Brody:

I'm a big fan of your boobs too, but getting you healthy is so much more important. Thinking of you!

Megan replied:

Brody, I liked that comment! My husband did not. He called it "inappropriate." Ha! Thanks though! (From me, not Danny.)

Monday, September 13, 2010
BANGS, BOOBS, AND BIOPSIES

I finally spoke with my oncologist and have the new and improved game plan for the next few weeks. First things first, my breast biopsy actually came back benign. While this is seemingly good news, the doctors are not putting much stock in this. Because the cyst was so big, the biopsy probably didn't retrieve the cancerous section with the needle. The fact that I have ovarian cancer and I'm twenty-eight (almost twenty-nine—birthday presents people!) still suggests that I have breast cancer.

Because at this point my ovarian cancer is more concerning than the breast, my doctors are going to proceed with a total abdominal hysterectomy with bilateral salpingo-oophorectomy. (Um, what? It just means they're removing my ovaries and uterus.) While doing that, they'll also perform a lumpectomy on my boob. What they find in the lumpectomy will determine how we deal with the breast cancer situation down the road.

Prior to this surgery, I'll also be undergoing some genetic testing, namely, being tested for a BRCA mutation that is potentially responsible for all of this.

Also, I'm going to get a second opinion. It looks like Danny and I are heading to Boston (pronounced Bah-Stan) or Houston, *y'all*! Time will tell which city and hospital we'll be gracing with our presence. I've tried my best to find some specialists in NYC (home of Top Shop) or Hawaii (no explanation needed—it's Hawaii!), but I seem to be coming up short.

I believe that's it for now. While I'm happy to have my hair for the time being, it breeds a whole new dilemma. I'm loving Rachel Berry's new bangs on Glee. I'm thinking about cutting mine. What do you guys think? I'm open to feedback.

5 COMMENTS

Stacie:
I thought you did have bangs? Are you thinking about a different type of bang? Please post pics if you get them.

Megan replied:
Stacie, I have a side sweep bang, which is completely different than Rachel Berry's bangs, which are more blunt and traditional. You just don't know because you have curly hair, making any sort of bang a bad decision for you, as we learned the hard way in high school. For the record, it wasn't *that* bad. Though clearly, it wasn't good.

Erin:

Megan, over the weekend I played Bananagrams. (If you haven't played it, you need to. It's like fast-paced Scrabble.) Anyway, I wanted to use your procedure title as a word. Of course, I couldn't think of that. (Only because I was drinking.) Instead I used "boob." Later I added an "s."

Uncle John:

Megan, don't worry about your hair. It will allow Danny to pretend like he's with a different woman.

Megan replied:

Uncle John, while you are probably right, you are still my uncle and therefore I think that's technically inappropriate for you to say. Nevertheless, I appreciate the encouragement. Love you!

Tuesday, September 14, 2010
OVARIAN CANCER AND ME

This morning I decided to look through some of the cancer literature my doctor gave me. I have lots of it: brochures, booklets, pamphlets, flyers, etc. I haven't wanted to look at this stuff until now because it makes this real. I don't want it to be real.

I have no interest in learning more about my disease. I've always been a believer in "ignorance is bliss." I don't want to know how many calories are in my Egg McMuffin. Nor do I want anyone taking a black light to my hotel bedspread. I sure as hell don't want to learn the definition of the imminent "transvaginal sonography" I'll be having. Just the words make me uncomfortable. I'm confident the definition will push me over the edge.

Nevertheless, I started my reading with a glossy blue booklet called "Ovarian Cancer Resource Guide for Newly-Diagnosed Women." It seemed like a good place to begin. I perused the pictures first. The first page showed a middle-aged woman doing what appeared to be abdominal work on a balance ball. I skipped to the next page: a couple on a mountainous hike. *Am I supposed to be working out?* I thought as flipped to the third picture of an Asian woman power walking. *Why are there all these pictures of women exercising? Is this the right booklet?*

The booklet also had a very useful section entitled "Questions to Ask Your Doctor." I couldn't help noticing how well thought out and comprehensive the list was. I sort of wished I'd had the courage to read this earlier and asked my doc some of this stuff, questions like:

- Have you treated other women with borderline tumors?
- Am I eligible for participation in clinical trials?
- Can you describe to me the staging process of cancer?

Instead, I quizzed my doctor with stuff that I just thought of on the fly:

- So, Stage 3 huh? Yikes. That's pretty bad, right?
- Have you heard of anyone beating this thing with V8? I was drinking a lot of V8 this afternoon.
- So, uh, that nurse that was in here earlier. She seemed nice, hey?

I still have a lot more reading to do. I'm saving "Ovarian Cancer and You" for tomorrow. I have a feeling that one is going to be pretty good. There's a picture of a woman sitting (as opposed to hiking) on the cover. That's more my cup of tea.

2 COMMENTS

Barbie:
Yeah, you're not a hiker. I'm not surprised you didn't like that particular pamphlet. I just wish I'd known that prior to selecting you as my hiking partner for the Inca Trail.

Megan replied:
Worst experience of my life, and yes, I'm aware I'm saying that on my cancer blog.

Wednesday, September 15, 2010
FERTILITY CENTER OF AMERICA

This morning Danny and I went to the Fertility Center of America. It was actually just down the street from our house, despite having such an official name. Fertility Center of America! Sounds so official and patriotic, no? Like it should be in Washington, DC, as opposed to the ghetto part of the city that it's actually in.

My gynecologist, not to be confused with my oncologist, scheduled this appointment for me. She thought I should speak with a fertility doctor to see if there was any way to preserve my fertility prior to undergoing the hysterectomy. This was actually my second fertility appointment within the past few days. The first fertility doctor told me I was not a candidate for any type of fertility treatment due to the location of my cancer.

The appointment started as they all do, with a catalog of paperwork. Though I must say, some of these questions were much more intriguing than normal. This paperwork, being a fertility clinic and all, was also interested in Danny.

13

Me: Honey, this has some questions on here for you too.

Danny: Okay.

Me: What's your social security number?

Danny: 357-34-1899.

Me: Okay. How many times do you masturbate per week?

Danny: *WHAT?!*

Me: I said, how many times do you masturbate per week?

Danny: What the fuck! I'm not answering that.

Me: Honey, you have to.

Danny: I'm not answering that.

Me: Fine. Next one. Do you experience pain after ejaculation?

Danny: *WHAT?! NO!*

Me: Honey, don't get upset. These are just questions to help us. Next one. On a scale from one to ten, how would you rate your wife as a lover?

Danny: It doesn't say that.

Me: Yes, it does. Now how would you rate your lover?

Danny: Ten.

Me: Good answer.

(It didn't say that.)

After the paperwork, I had a plethora of ultrasounds taken, which was the last thing I wanted to do. The ultrasounds were mandatory, though. I know because I asked the nurse if I "had to" and she said "yes." After doing that, Danny and I finally sat down with the doctor, who broke down the fertility game plan. Basically, this fertility doctor wants to put me on a bunch of fertility drugs to fatten up my eggs. Once they are nice and fat and easy to retrieve, she'd do just that. Retrieve them and freeze them so I would have them down the road.

So that's what Danny and I are supposed to be thinking over: if we want to pursue fertility treatment prior to the hysterectomy.

We're not thinking very hard about it though, because we don't. I've been a patient enough lately and I like to think I've been a good sport about it. The last thing I want to do is go to a fertility clinic, every day, for the next thirty days to be poked and prodded more. Not to mention the risks.

Fertility treatment involves sticking a needle into a patient's ovary—and in my case, into the cancer. When you stick a needle in an ovary, tiny particles of the ovary are often displaced into the abdomen. For a woman with normal ovaries, this isn't a big deal. But for me it wouldn't be just the ovary particles being spread, but possibly the cancer as well. And spreading cancer is a bad thing. You don't have to be a doctor to know that. (Though I do have my PhD: Player Hating Degree!)

So that's that. I, Megan Silianoff, will never be able to have children. It's heavy. Very heavy. I mean, I one hundred percent always saw kids in my future. Danny did too. We even know what we'd name a girl if we had one (and a boy, for that matter: since Danny is a junior, we'd have to carry on that tradition with our son). I mean, we haven't been trying or anything, but it was definitely something we saw down the road, sooner rather than later.

I think I'm numb to this infertility sentence though. I have too much going on to properly mourn that specific aspect of this mess. Or maybe my perspective is too skewed. A week ago, I didn't know if I was going to live. I really didn't. It's not like my doctor said, "You are going to die." Or, "You have six months to live." And I was too scared to ask. So I'm still in a place where any side effect that's not death is a positive, even if that side effect happens to be the death of my fertility.

Besides, there is always adoption, right? Do you guys know Lily from *Modern Family*? I'd love a little Asian baby just like her. Because I'm sure adoption is just that easy, right? "Uh, Adoption People? Hi. This is Megan. Do you have any Lilys? Really? Great!"

1 COMMENT

Aaron:

Megan, I've secretly been creeping on here hoping that everything would turn in your fortune and I wouldn't have to create a log-in. I figure now that you're going to be kicking cancer's ass, I could, at the very least, create a password and write something.

Friday, September 17, 2010
BOSTON

I'm in Boston, people! Home of *Cheers*. Home of Harvard. Home of . . . I don't know what else. J. Crew, maybe? People *really* are preppy here—that stereotype is true for sure! Unfortunately, however, Boston didn't bring the closure I was hoping it would. I suppose my ideal scenario would have gone something like this:

> **Boston Doctors:** Let us start, Megan, by saying, cute outfit.
> **Me:** Really? Thanks!
> **Boston Doctors:** Well, Megan, we Boston Doctors recommend the identical procedure your Chicago Doctors have proposed. We agree with every minor detail of your diagnosis and treatment plan. Hats off to you for assembling such a great team of medical professionals!
> **Me:** Why, thank you!
> **Boston Doctors:** Now, would you like us to write you a prescription for more painkillers? We realize the pain from your surgery is probably subsiding, but they are always good for recreational use.
> **Me:** I suppose. If you insist!

But that's not what happened. The Boston doctors seem to have two points of contention with my existing diagnosis. The first being that they don't think I have breast cancer! Obviously, amazing! But also very confusing.

The second difference of opinion arose when discussing chemotherapy. Basically, the Boston doctors think it's unnecessary. Without getting all textbook, the doctor basically said that my cancer is lazy. (Ha! Of course! How apropos.)

My type of cancer doesn't spread quickly—maybe never at all. It tends to be unresponsive to chemotherapy, so they don't see a point in doing it. My doctor explained that, in his opinion, the only way to effectively cure this type of cancer is to surgically remove it every time it returns. Or, as he phrased it, "cut it out." It was at this point that I laughed and did the Joey Gladstone/*Full House* scissors bit. Both my mom and Danny immediately glared at me. Tough crowd.

So that's where we're at. Whether or not I have breast cancer is still up in the air—as is my fate with chemo. It's almost as if we took two steps backward as opposed to one step forward. Although what Boston is telling me is potentially good news, I need to get some solidarity on my diagnosis to know for sure.

This is why I've decided to postpone my scheduled surgery in Chicago. Danny and I will go to Houston in two weeks for a third, and hopefully tie-breaking, opinion. Obviously we'd like to go right away, but two weeks out is the quickest appointment we could get. MD Anderson Cancer Center, the hospital I'll be attending, is supposed to be the best in the nation. So I'm feeling fortunate that I got an appointment at all. That's it for now, *y'all*.

2 COMMENTS

Dad:
So I did that breast cancer walk for nothing?

Megan replied:
Nice, Dad. Real nice.

Tuesday, September 21, 2010
KELSEY MORGAN STAFFING COMPANY

Home sweet home. After spending the weekend in Boston, I'm back home in Chicago. I have over a week before I leave for Houston, so I decided there was no reason not to go to work today. I feel fine physically. Plus, it enables me to see my dad and brother, as I'm the recruiting manager for our family business, a staffing company called Kelsey Morgan Staffing.

My dad started Kelsey Morgan almost twenty years ago. Prior to that he'd been in the beer business working for Budweiser, which I suppose was technically Anheuser-Busch. He started right out of college as a route salesman and eventually worked his way up to middle management. The fact that my dad worked for Budweiser made for what I suspect are unique childhood memories. The year I rode in the "Bud Mobile" for our town's Fourth of July parade comes to mind. My dad drove the car, Spuds MacKenzie and I shared shotgun, all while three bikini-clad "Bud Girls" threw candy from the backseat. What? You guys didn't do that too?

I also have vivid memories of my dad teaching my younger brother and me how to operate the kegerator that he'd installed. He kept it in our family room so that my brother, Ryan, and

I could serve him and his friends perfectly poured beers. My brother was barely out of diapers yet could pour a Bud Light with virtually no foam.

Eventually my dad began to tire of the beer business. (Or, more likely, my mom did! Looking back on it now, I'm assuming an occupational hazard of the beer business is frequent inebriation.) My dad's best friend at the time had his own staffing company and wanted my dad to open a sister branch. My dad knew nothing about staffing back then; no one did, it was still a relatively new industry. But his friend assured him that "as long as you can sell" he'd land on his feet. And my dad can sell. He's the ultimate salesman: charismatic, funny, and confident. He can sell ice to an Eskimo! Ketchup to a guy in a white shirt! Babies to the Octomom!

Because of his sales skills, my dad's friend was right, and he was able to obtain enough clients that Kelsey Morgan's debut was a success. Today Kelsey Morgan Staffing is a thriving company that employs me, my brother, twelve internal employees, and Booker. (Booker is the official company mascot. Though we're currently in negotiations about his pay.)

There are a lot of great things about working in the family business. Take what's happening to me right now, for example. I haven't been to work for over three weeks now, for all of which I've been paid. I assume if I were working for another company not owned by my father I'd have to quit or take a leave of absence at the very least.

More than that, I like the idea of working with my younger brother to help build the company my dad started. I think there is something romantic about that. (Working with my brother is not romantic. But the idea of us, the second generation, building upon something the first generation built is. Let's make sure that distinction is clear.)

Also, for the first time since graduating from college, I have a job that I'm really invested in, where I don't just go through the motions. I take pride in overseeing the company's recruiting efforts and like to think I'm good at it. Because I worked at a staffing company before (the one where I met Danny!), I've been able to apply a lot of that gained knowledge and experience to what we do at Kelsey. Before my brother and I came around, my dad didn't have many company systems, policies, or structure of any kind. As he puts it, he did a lot of "shooting from the hip."

All that said, working with your family can be very trying at times. I submit expense reports to my mom, who likes to audit me on every single thing. You should hear the horror in her voice when I tell her, "No, Ma! I didn't use a coupon at Office Depot." And disagreements with my brother are never really about the issue at hand; they always have deeper subtext, like who got better Christmas gifts in '92. Or who Grandma liked better. (Though I'm pretty sure she disliked us both equally.)

And then there's my dad. Love that guy! Love him to death! But he comes with special idiosyncrasies that often make me say, *Dad—what?!* Let me give you an example.

My dad often cooks breakfast for our offices, usually on Fridays. We have a kitchen in both office locations, so making breakfast isn't much of a distraction to our recruiters, who could potentially be interviewing candidates at the given time. Once my dad was slaving away in the kitchen, overseeing the sausage, pancakes, and bacon he had going on the griddle. Apparently ready to fire the eggs, and unaware of what anyone else might be doing at the time, he yelled from the kitchen, "HEY MARE! HOW DO YOU WANT YOUR EGGS?!"

Mary, a recruiter, was not sure how to integrate her egg order into the interview she was conducting. "OVER EASY!" she responded to my dad sheepishly, loud enough that he could make it out in the other room.

"JUST HOW I LIKE MY WOMAN!" he hollered back and proceeded to crack himself up for all of us to hear.

The candidate's facial expression was priceless.

But that's my dad. You never know what's going to come out of that mouth of his. While many clients *love* my dad, there are a few who aren't fans. In the early 90s, my dad decided to experiment with some aggressive marketing tactics and started a monthly direct mail campaign. One particular month he sent out a letter from the perspective of our family dog, asking prospective clients to "throw my dad a bone." Cute. The next month he sent out a roll of Lifesavers saying that Kelsey Morgan could be your "lifesaver." Sorta corny, but it was the 90s and the whole wordplay with candy stuff was big. Then the third month came and he sent out what I call the "marketing letter heard 'round the world." My colleagues more commonly refer to it as "the sex letter." My dad basically sent out a letter claiming that if you hired Kelsey Morgan, you'd be happier, and therefore have a better sex life. *Dad, what?!*

Needless to say, Kelsey Morgan got a lot of calls that day from people asking to be removed from the mailing list. Ten years later, our marketing efforts are still somewhat coming from a place of damage control. Love that guy though.

Today at work, however, has been weird, as I haven't much to do. (With the exception of teaching my dad how to "copy and paste" on his computer, which was huge.) Having been out of the office for so long, I'm completely out of the loop. Usually my days consist of conducting five or six interviews, but today I obviously had none scheduled. I've helped my colleague, Sean, by editing résumés for some his candidates, but even that didn't take more than a few minutes. It did, however, inspire me to make one additional résumé: mine! Just for fun.

Making my résumé, however, proved to be harder than anticipated. Including Kelsey Morgan, I've had three jobs since graduating college. This is seven professional years to account for. The problem is that I can barely remember what my "responsibilities" were at my previous positions. Ironically, I remember all the dicking around I did like it was yesterday. So I decided to create my résumé with all this latter stuff, which I think proved to be much more entertaining. So without further ado, enjoy.

MEGAN SILIANOFF
1555 Huron Street,
Chicago, IL 414.405.4889

PROFESSIONAL EXPERIENCE
Copier Business Solutions
Chicago, Illinois
(July 2004–December 2005)
Account Representative

- Knew shockingly little information about the copiers I was supposed to be selling.
- Left the office every day to conduct "cold calls."
- "Cold called" nail salons, movie theaters, restaurants, my bed, Michigan Avenue, and other places as I saw fit.
- Flirted with male colleagues I deemed attractive and fun.
- Took regular afternoon breaks at the convenience store in our building where I purchased candy and browsed celebrity gossip magazines.
- Routinely fell short of the monthly quota of $33,500 worth of copier equipment.

The Recruiting Group
Chicago, Illinois
(December 2005–September 2007)
Direct Hire Recruiter

- Cried at my desk the first day upon realizing I couldn't leave the office and really had to work.
- Went to Starbucks two to three times a day.
- Routinely served as a distraction to the entire organization due to personal issues revolving around my romantic life.
- Met and later ended up marrying a client. (Danny!)
- Spent the last hour of each day snacking on pretzels and conversing with colleagues about their plans for the evening.

Kelsey Morgan Staffing Company
Chicago, Illinois
(September 2007–Present)
Recruiting Manager

- Interview sexual offenders, convicts, and all types of felons on a daily basis.
- Regularly kick homeless people out of our office during the winter, informing them that we aren't a safe haven from the cold.
- Recruited for a position in which shoveling worm manure was a core aspect of the job.
- Fight with my brother regarding most aspects of our business, routinely utilizing the words "fuck," "motherfucker," and "asshole" during said debates.
- Make daily trips to Walgreens where every Walgreens employee knows me by name.
- Discovered, utilized, and fell in love with Facebook. Enough said.

EDUCATION

Augustana College
Rock Island, Illinois

- **Bachelors of Arts in Speech Communication,** *I was originally a business major but had to switch as I couldn't pass accounting.*
- **Bachelors of Arts in Spanish,** *It's shocking and sad how little Spanish I can actually speak.*
- **Concentration in Latin American Studies,** *Ironically I can locate neither Venezuela nor Paraguay on a map!*
- **Semester Abroad in Latin America** *(Partying)*
- **Summers Abroad in Cuenca, Ecuador, at CEDEI School and London, England, at AIU University** *(Partying)*

2 COMMENTS

Danielle:
Hahaha! As a colleague of Megan's at the Recruiting Group, I can vouch for all of those "responsibilities."

Megan replied:
References!

Wednesday, September 22, 2010
"M" AS IN "MEGAN"

I've started packing for Houston. I'm not entirely sure how long I'll be down there, so the contents of my suitcase are pretty random. (My suitcase has nude pantyhose in it. I didn't even know I owned nude pantyhose. I came across them while packing and thought, *Nude pantyhose? Weird! I'm bringing these to Houston!*) What I do know, however, is the patient coordinator at MD Anderson thinks I'm stupid. She's probably right.

She simply needed me to verify the spelling of my last name over the phone. That shouldn't be hard. However, I'm terrible at spelling anything with phonetic examples. You know what I mean? Like, *V* as in Victor. *R* as in Roger. I freeze up and can't think of anything appropriate whenever I'm expected to participate in this type of banter.

Patient Coordinator: So that's Silianoff, ma'am?

Me: Yep!

Patient Coordinator: Can you go ahead and spell that for me, ma'am, just to confirm?

Me: Uh, sure. S-I-L-I-A-N-O-F-F.

Patient Coordinator: Can you spell that again for me with phonetic examples, ma'am? Just to ensure accuracy.

Me: Uh. Okay. Yeah. *S* as in snakes. *I* as in ice cream. *L* as in Lady Gaga. (Then I started laughing.) Sorry, ma'am. I don't know why I said that. It's just the first thing that popped in my head that started with an *L*. Sorry! (Still laughing.)

Patient Coordinator: It's okay, Ms. Silianoff. Please continue.

Me: *I* as in ice cube. (*The rapper,* I thought. But remembered this woman didn't need context.) *A* as in apple. *N* as in no. *O* as in octopus. *F* as in for sure. *F* as in for sure.

Patient Coordinator: Wow. Okay, Mrs. Silianoff. We'll see you in two weeks.

So like I said, I'm stupid. But in my defense, this is 2010. You think I'd be able to register online, right?

3 COMMENTS

Danny:
Sure, but you are still stupid.

Mom:
D as in "dumb."

Megan replied:
Whatever. You guys are rude. I have cancer.

Friday, September 24, 2010
GENETIC COUNSELING

Today I spent the afternoon at a genetic counselor's office. Her name was Cara and she was nice, tall, thin, and vaguely resembled Hilary Swank. Her office was small, but her candy bowl was big—overflowing with fun-size Twix bars. I took this as an open invitation to help myself.

Prior to our session, I wasn't real clear on what a genetic counselor did or why I was going. I just knew my doctor had scheduled this appointment and I had to attend. I guess, though, with the word counselor in her title, I'd envisioned myself doing the majority of the talking—a very Robin Williams/Matt Damon/*Good Will Hunting* type of situation. I want everyone to know that is not what genetic counseling is. Genetic counseling is when Cara describes to you, in full detail, every gene, cancer, mutation, and horrific disease that I could possibly possess or develop in my life. And there's a lot. Like millions.

It was very overwhelming and very scary. My first instinct was to jump from the fourteenth floor that we were on to alleviate the suspense surrounding my eventual cause of death. Instead, I let Cara perform a blood test for the millions of genetic disorders we discussed in our session. In two to three weeks I'll know if I have the BRCA 1 or 2 mutations that my doctors are most concerned about. Testing positive for the BRCA 1 or 2 gene means that I will very likely develop *both* ovarian cancer and breast cancer in my lifetime. (If I haven't already.)

The BRCA gene is hereditary and would have been passed down from either my mother or father. If I have this, I'll want to make sure that my younger female cousins, from whichever side the gene was contracted, get tested as well. Since the gene is hereditary, if I have it, they could have it too. If I had a sister, she would need to get tested too.

I also asked Cara to test for the "crazy" gene. I'm pretty sure I have that.

Monday, September 27, 2010
BON VOYAGE

We leave for Houston this week. I have no idea when I'll be back but I do know that I plan to be poolside for the majority of the trip. How did I end up with ovarian cancer and not skin cancer? It's like God doesn't know me at all. Have a good weekend, everybody!

3 COMMENTS

Anne-Marie:

I, too, am shocked you don't have skin cancer. I've never seen someone so passionate about their hatred for sunscreen.

Megan replied:

It's not that I *hate* sunscreen. It's more that I *love* being tan. Do you see the difference?

Anne-Marie replied:

For the sake of not having this conversation again, I'm going to say that I do.

Friday, October 1, 2010
GREETINGS FROM TEXAS!

The drama continues, *y'all*. November 1 is D-Day. I've decided to have surgery in Houston. The doctor here seemed, by far, the most experienced regarding my specific type of cancer. (Which is "serous borderline tumors." Also called "low malignant potential." I don't know if I've officially said that yet.) Dr. Bear sees patients like me weekly, while my doctor in Chicago seemed to regard my case as very rare. And get this: My doctor in Chicago did her residency for my doctor here in Houston. So now I'm essentially seeing the teacher of all the students. That's an upgrade, right? Therefore deciding to have surgery here in Houston, with this doctor, was an easy choice to make. Especially when you hear this next part.

My surgery will be one of suspense. Dr. Bear is going to make decisions on what body parts she needs to extract while

I'm on the table, depending on how much cancer she finds. It could be everything, including ovaries, uterus, and other stuff. Or it could be nothing. Most likely, it will be somewhere between those extremes. Time will tell.

It does look like I'm on the no chemo plan, however, which is fantastic! My doctor here agrees with my doctor in Boston. The specific cancer I have tends to be unresponsive to chemotherapy. Therefore, there is no point in putting me through it. To which I responded, "*Totally*!"

There is more great news, if you can believe it! The doctors here agree with the doctors in Boston regarding my breast cancer. Or should I say, the lack thereof? They too, based on my biopsy results, don't think I have breast cancer! How great is that? They want to monitor the cyst very closely but don't see a need to remove it at the time being.

While all of this is phenomenal news, and I don't want to dwell on the negative, I can't help being slightly annoyed at the doctors in Chicago. I mean, who tells someone they have breast cancer if they don't? Rude.

So to sum up:
1. I'm having surgery November 1.
2. I'm not doing chemo.
3. I don't have breast cancer.
4. I am pumped!

4 COMMENTS

Dad:
November 1? Well that's going to work out pretty good!

29

Megan replied:
Why?

Dad replied:
That's bye week for the Bears!

Megan replied:
Good, Dad. I'm happy for you.

Saturday, October 2, 2010
HOUSTON, TEXAS, USA

Houston continues to be a successful trip. Not only have I gotten a treatment plan in place, found a doctor I trust, and received favorable news regarding my prognosis, I have also become acquainted with my new city of residence! (Cue gasp!)

My husband is a flourishing businessman and his job is taking us to Houston. We've actually known we were moving to Houston for a week or two before I was diagnosed, but were just processing it ourselves before really telling our friends and family. The war on cancer, however, intervened, so the move is on the backburner until we know what is going on with me.

For those of you who don't know what Danny does, join the club. I know it involves law firms, software, and frequent trips to Joseph A. Banks. If you ask me to explain it further than that, I'm going to use the word "um" frequently and rely heavily on buzz words which is my go-to way of explaining it. My explanations usually go like this:

Random Person: What does your husband do for a living, Megan?

Me: Oh. Uh. Well you know Enron? He does that, basically.

Random Person: He is a white-collar criminal? (Surprised)

Me: No! He, like, seizes computers so they can be investigated for white-collar crime. You know, like electronic discovery? For like law firms and stuff? You know?

Random Person: Uh . . .

Me: Let's change the subject.

Danny's company offered him a great opportunity to do whatever it is that he does now, and more, in Houston, where the company is based. Not only will he have more opportunities, but now he'll no longer have to work remotely from home, which we both don't love. Danny doesn't like it because he's such a social person. He benefits deeply from going into an office every day and talking to his colleagues about sports or whatever water cooler stuff guys talk about. I can't imagine it's much other than sports.

From my perspective, I don't like Danny working from home because it's difficult for him to turn off the IT switch at the end of the day. I encourage him to get his IT on all day long, but when the clock strikes five, he needs to speak English (or urban slang, which I'm a fan of as well!) and not this gigabyte language that he's so fluent in. It actually became so much of a problem in the past that we had to make a marital compromise. In exchange for Danny not speaking "Gigabyte" language, I had to stop saying I wanted to get things "poppin." And calling Danny a cracker.

It's possible that I've digressed. Let me try again. We're moving to Houston. I'm definitely sad. Telling my family that I was not only moving away from them, but also the family business, was one of the hardest, most emotional things I have had to do. I had to get drunk just to do it—and subsequently they all had to get drunk just to bear it. It was awful. (Though deep into the night, after we couldn't cry anymore, it did get kinda fun due to the collaborative drunkeness!)

But when I stop thinking about that "leaving my family" aspect of moving, I actually get really excited. I've lived in the Midwest my entire life, so it will be good for me to experience something new. Plus the weather in Chicago blows. No more snow, no more monotonous gray skies, no more shoveling my car out in the street just so I can go to the grocery store. (Or watching Danny do it.)

Not to mention the unbelievable coincidence that MD Anderson is located in Houston. I mean, sure, knowing that we were eventually moving to Houston played a small role in deciding to go there, as opposed to somewhere else, for the third opinion. But it's very likely that I would have come here regardless, as it's the best in the world. I'm so lucky for this uncanny coincidence.

2 COMMENTS

Cara:
I remember asking you "what your husband did" the very first time I met you. You told me he "does stuff with paper."

Megan replied:
I stand by that explanation.

Sunday, October 3, 2010
CONCERNS ABOUT HOUSTON, TEXAS, USA

When Danny and I aren't at MD Anderson, we've been staking out the city for points of interest for our impending move. I've already established key things, like where I'll get my hair cut. And the shopping scene looks doable. There is a neighborhood called River Oaks that I'm especially fond of because it reminds me of my favorite domestic city, Malibu. I've actually never been to Malibu, but I know I love it. As the chubby nun in *Sister Act 2* says, "You don't have to taste the donut to know it's sweet." (*Sister Act 2: Back in the Habit* is my all-time favorite movie. Shout out to Sister Mary Clarence!)

Anyway, there are also some points of concern regarding Houston, which I'd like to share with you now.

MEGAN'S CONCERNS ABOUT HOUSTON, TEXAS, USA

Kolaches
Most of you probably don't know what a kolache is because you, like me, are a Yankee. I'm here to tell you that a kolache is essentially a dinner roll with breakfast food stuffed inside it: meat, egg, cheese, sausage, bacon. Danny is a huge fan. I am skeptical. Though if they wanted to do something with chocolate inside, I can see myself coming around quite quickly.

Dunkin' Donuts
From what I can tell, there are no Dunkin' Donuts in Houston or the surrounding Houston area. Because Dunkin' Donuts is my favorite, and an integral part of my morning routine, I'm gravely concerned. I'd like to take this opportunity to encourage everyone reading this to consider opening a Dunkin' Donuts franchise in the greater Houston area. I can commit to daily patronage right here, right now.

The Rodeo
There's a lot of talk and general excitement about the rodeo here. While I'm trying to keep an open mind about this event, I'm failing and continue to think it's for hicks.

NASA
This isn't so much a concern, as much as it's a desire. I think the prospect of me working at NASA is fantastic. Granted I'd probably have to be a receptionist or a janitor, but it would still enable me to have a conversation such as the following:

Random Person: So what do you do for work, Megan?
Me: Oh, me? I work at NASA.
Random Person: Wow. Really? How impressive.
Me: I know.

Houston Geography
Driving is not one of my strengths, though I will say that I've only been in one car accident in my lifetime. And that accident had a lot more to do with texting than it did driving. Nevertheless, my bad driving paired with my bad sense of direction is going to be a rough combo when trying to navigate a new city. The positive, however, is that Houston has an HOV lane on the freeway.

Though Danny insists this is an acronym for "high occupancy vehicle," I know that he is a liar. It's obviously a nod to Jay-Z and I love Houston for it. ("Hov" is a derivative of "Jehovah," which means God. Jay-Z's often called "Hov" because he considers himself to be the god of rap, as do I.)

Monday, October 4, 2010
WHAT I LEARNED TODAY

Today I learned a very valuable lesson while at a Barnes & Noble bookstore in Houston. Though this lesson has nothing to do with cancer per se, I still found it insightful and want all of you to benefit from this life lesson that I have learned.

What I learned today is that if you see a toddler, alone, in Barnes & Noble, you should not automatically assume they have been abandoned. Furthermore, you should not pick up said child and begin carrying them to customer service. Should you do this, a mother will soon notice her missing child and scream, "STOP! KIDNAPPER! STOP!" as you ride down the escalator with her child. This is highly embarrassing and, in my experience, provokes the toddler to cry.

What I learned today (with the help of Barnes & Noble security) is that if you see a toddler alone in Barnes & Noble, you should survey the scene for a nearby parent. You should survey the scene for more than "like a second," which is the amount of time I testified to looking. Barnes & Noble's official recommendation is to wait with the child until a parent surfaces, as they apparently "always do." According to Barnes & Noble personnel, "No child in the history of the fifteen years we've been in this location has been abandoned." As I told them, I did not know that.

Wednesday, October 6, 2010
AUNT MEGAN

A great thing about having surgery in Houston and moving here is that Danny has family nearby. Therefore, Danny and I are spending a day or two with his sister and niece prior to going home to Chicago.

Marrying Danny made me an instant aunt. This is a title I enjoy and a role I strive to be good at. Danny's family is huge and there are a few second marriages involved, so I believe I have roughly thirteen, maybe fourteen, nieces and nephews. (Though a good aunt probably doesn't use the word "roughly" and knows the exact number.)

This weekend I'm spending quality time with my fifth-grade niece, Jessie. She and I have always gotten along well. I'm starting to realize, after being BFFs this weekend, that maybe we get along *too* well. The following is a list of commonalities I've discovered thus far:

COMMONALTIES BETWEEN ME AND MY ELEVEN-YEAR-OLD NIECE

1. Our iPods have an abundance of ~~Kesha~~ . . . Ke$ha.
2. We both struggle to pay attention in church.
3. We both find it hilarious when someone's cell phone goes off in church. (Though in my case, I had to confirm it wasn't mine. But then, like I said, hilarious!)
4. We both have a friend named Erica who has her ears pierced!
5. We both want our mom to buy us an iPhone.
6. We both like Frito pie. (I've actually never had Frito Pie, but I'm confident it's my favorite "hot lunch" too, just based on the name.)

7. We both want to be fashion designers when we grow up.

This list is a tad on the lengthy side given our age difference. But if that means I get to start eating Frito pie on a regular basis, I'm fine with it.

Friday, October 8, 2010
TEST RESULTS

I heard from Cara, my genetic counselor, today. It appears my genetic shortcomings are limited to the areas I'm already aware of: height, math, and math. (Seriously, I'm really bad.) I have tested negatively for the BRCA 1 and 2 mutations, so that is fantastic! Shout out to my ancestors in Ireland and Italy for passing down legit DNA.

3 COMMENTS

Barbie:
Megan, great news! You are really bad at math though. Remember at Piece Pizza when you tipped the waitress like fifty bucks because you couldn't figure out 20 percent?

Janelle:
Ha! I remember that. I also remember junior year business statistics class. That was just hard to watch. You really are bad at math.

Megan replied:
Hey, guys! While I love the participation and commenting on my blog, let's try to keep it encouraging, shall we? This isn't a roast. I

have cancer, you bitches! Love you though! And stats class, holy shit. You aren't lying.

Friday, October 8, 2010
E-MAIL CORRESPONDENCE

From: megan@hotmail.com
To: Extended Family Distribution List
Subject: Family Genetics

Good news, Family!

It appears our genetic shortcomings are limited to the areas we're already aware of: alcohol, tasteless humor, rosacea, and the lower half of our bodies resembling that of a pear. I have tested negatively for the BRCA 1 and 2 mutations. Therefore, none of my beautiful cousins have anything to worry about, with regard to this particular issue anyway. (See previously mentioned genetic shortcomings.)

See you at Thanksgiving!

~Megan

Monday, October 11, 2010
CHECKING MY VOICE MAIL

I hate talking on the phone. I hate it a lot. It's not a reflection of my feelings for the caller. I'm just not a phone person. Even more than that, I hate checking my voice mails. And because I rarely answer my phone, I constantly have an abundance of them.

My new circumstances, however, of having doctors, hospitals, pharmacies, insurance companies, and other cancer-related parties constantly blowing me up has changed things. This has forced me to pick up my phone more frequently. Or at the very least, listen to my voice mails.

So this morning I channeled all my willpower and checked all eight of my voice mails. Instead of calling everyone back, however, I've decided to address the callers in this open forum. I hope no one minds, but I think this will be more efficient.

TO THE PEOPLE WHO LEFT ME VOICE MAILS

Aunt Debbie:
Thanks for the birthday wishes! It feels good to be twenty-eight. Although by now, I'm closer to twenty-nine. And that's not as ideal.

Mom:
No, I don't think Danny wants a blender for his birthday. But now that we have one, we use it. I swear!

Danny:
We drink skim milk in our house. You, as we know, picked up 2 percent.

Doctor's Office:
Yes, I am aware of our appointment on October 30, 2010 at 10:45 a.m. For the record, I'm still in a lot of "general pain" if you want to change your mind about any of those prescriptions I asked for.

Blockbuster:

WTF! I thought you had "no late fees." What do you mean you're automatically deducting from my debit account? This is bullshit.

My dear friend, Eric Johnston:

Yes, I see the irony in you responding to my text, "Yay! You finally got text messaging!" with a phone call. I see the irony indeed.

Julianna:

No, I don't know of a good hair salon in Bucktown. Unfortunately I know tons of bad ones. Let me know if you want the names of those.

Monday, October 18, 2010
BOOK DRIVE

I'd like to take this opportunity to give a shout to Erin Doucette, my former high school English teacher, for organizing a book drive in my honor at Franklin High School. (My alma mater! Go Sabers!) Erin and I were very close throughout my high school career. Part of the reason was that she wasn't *that* much older than me at the time—she was right out of college and in her early twenties. Plus, Erin wasn't *just* my teacher, but my volleyball coach and my employer! (Of sorts.) Senior year I was Erin's "teacher's aide." As her aide, I was supposed to help her grade papers, make photocopies, and things of that nature. I don't remember doing those things as much as trying to set her up with all the eligible bachelors in the math and physical education departments. Not that she asked me to do any matchmaking, but this was the pre-online dating era (think more Y2K!) and I just wanted to make sure my girl had a special somebody with whom she could attend prom (as chaperones).

Anyway, Erin heard about my cancer and asked if she could organize a book drive in my honor. She knows that I'm an avid reader (as is she, being an English teacher and all) and she thought having my own "library" while I recover would be nice. So sweet, right? Easy to see why she was my favorite teacher.

So this is my formal SHOUT OUT and THANK YOU to all you who donated books to me at Franklin High School!

Going through all the boxes of books to see what I had scored was amazing. Truly. But what I enjoyed even more was watching my friend Ann carry five boxes of books up my two flights of stairs. Ann's mom works at the high school, which is how she was selected as the designated courier. I haven't seen Ann work so hard or sweat so much since we were on the high school basketball team sophomore year. (This hard work being precisely the reason we quit basketball.)

Anyway, I now have my own personal library and I'm really excited about the books that await me. Not to mention a lot of these books came with really sweet cards or notes from past teachers or faculty at the high school. There were, however, a few contributions (all of them conveniently anonymous) that I found interesting and am going to share with you now.

INTERESTING BOOK CONTRIBUTIONS FROM FRANKLIN HIGH SCHOOL

When Things Fall Apart: Heart Advice for Difficult Times
Topical, sure, but sorta depressing, no? I got bummed out just reading the title.

The Holy Bible

A classic about a young, tenacious Jewish boy named Jesus. Thank you, whoever gave this to me!

My Sister's Keeper

For those who don't know, *My Sister's Keeper* is a book by Jodi Picoult about a young girl who has cancer and ends up dying. Um, thanks? I guess? Whoever contributed this book—you shouldn't have! No, really!

3 COMMENTS

Heather:

I remember when Ann played basketball. Wasn't she super good?

Megan replied:

Indeed. Ann was super good at basketball. She was on varsity as a freshman. But like me, between underage drinking and experimental marijuana use, she didn't have time for extracurricular activities.

Mom:

Come on, Megan. My friends read this.

Thursday, October 28, 2010
MASSAGE GONE WRONG

Danny and I have arrived safely in Houston. My surgery is in seventy-two hours. We're just trying to relax and stay busy so we're not sitting around thinking about it. This is why I decided to get a massage today and Danny decided to play a quick round of golf.

I wasn't envisioning anything fancy in terms of my massage experience. Just a quick, cheap chair massage was all I had in mind. I remembered seeing a nail salon that looked decent last time we were here, so I decided to try it. I told the Asian lady behind the counter that I wanted a massage.

She gave me a nasty look and said in a thick accent, "Don't do massage. Just manicure and pedicure."

"Huh," I said. "I guess I was confused by the neon sign on your window that says *massage*." I turned around and looked to ensure that the sign was still there. (It was.)

I decided to try somewhere with a more explicit name and business model. I drove over to Massage Heaven, a massage chain that appears to be popular in Houston. I knew I was in trouble upon meeting my massage therapist. He looked like a Greek Danny DeVito.

I took off my shirt and got into the bed. My massage began, as did the talking. Talking, talking, talking. Danny DeVito gabbed throughout the entirety of my massage. Though I have a lot to choose from, these were some of my favorite conversation starters/observations that Mr. DeVito dazzled me with:

- "You need to eat more protein. Not red meat, but perhaps wild cod. As long as it's not farm raised. Do you like cod?"
- "Do you feel anything?"
- "Does it feel good?"
- "You are very flexible."
- "Don't eat sugar after 3:00 p.m. Do you eat sugar after 3:00 p.m.?"
- "You need to be stronger. This is the most important thing in life."

The random observations and bizarre questions stopped only when he started trying to schedule my next appointment. Right there on the spot. Because what's more relaxing than a high-pressure sales pitch?

Sunday, October 31, 2010
SHOWTIME

My surgery is tomorrow at 3:00 p.m. I'm kinda dreading it, but it will also be nice to get it over with.

Change your thoughts and you've changed your life. I saw a knick-knack in a store the other day with this saying and it really resonated with me. I find the whole concept extremely liberating. Perspective has been my most useful tool throughout these past two months, more so than God, faith, or anything else people cling to in times of crisis.

I hope that no one feels bad for me, because I don't feel bad for myself. There are way too many bald kids roaming the halls of this hospital to even flirt with that sentiment. There is nothing that can happen tomorrow that won't make me feel fortunate about my lot in life. Not being able to have children, menopause at twenty-eight, the cancer spreading more than anticipated—all small potatoes. If these are the worst things that happen in my life, I'm fortunate.

I can think of so many people and so many situations direr than mine. My cousin died fighting for his country in Afghanistan when he was nineteen. September 11 comes to mind. These horrific school shootings. These are real tragedies. A twenty-eight-year-old with a little ovarian cancer fails miserably in comparison to these things. How good you have it is just a matter of perspective, is it not?

Nevertheless, thanks for everyone's prayers and well-wishes. The support has been a welcome and helpful distraction. My mom or Danny will update the blog once I'm out of surgery to let everyone know what went down. Word to the wise, Linda Halpin, my mother, will WebMD your ass before you even know what hit you. She's not afraid of medical terminology or Internet research. This makes for a lethal and long-winded combination. I'd start reading any type of science-related text you have now to prepare. The periodic table of elements has proved helpful to me in the past. Danny, on the other hand, is dyslexic. So either way, you guys are in for it.

I promise I'll write again one day soon! Love you all!

2 COMMENTS

Marc:

Hang in there, Megs! You're doing great. I told Danny he has to take you to Maui for a month once you're feeling better. What's his credit card number? I'll get on www.Priceline.com and get the ball rolling. We love you! Thinking of you!

Megan replied:

Marc, I just texted it to you. Good looking out! Get something with an ocean view.

Monday, November 1, 2010
SURGERY UPDATE

Hey everyone, it's Danny. Here is the update. I'm going to keep this fairly short. I'm not the writer or speller in the family, so please bear with me.

To start, thank you for all your texts, e-mails, and overall well-wishes this morning as Megan went into surgery. They were tremendously comforting and help set the attitude Megan needed to tackle this day.

We witnessed a true miracle this afternoon. Megan's doctor completed the surgery around 4:30 p.m. She informed us that she only removed the left ovary and that the right ovary was salvageable. During the surgery she noticed that Megan's bladder was tipped over onto her uterus and fixed its position accordingly. This is likely responsible for the pain Megan has experienced for quite some time—the pain that led Megan to go to the doctor in the first place. (Not that she'd ever mention the fact that she was in pain to anyone.) Megan's doctor also explored the areas she felt the cancer was most likely to spread to. She debulked (a.k.a. removed) the cancer from those areas and now believes all the cancer is gone.

Megan is in a lot of pain, but she'll get through it. It looks like she'll be in the hospital for four to five more days. We hope to be in Chicago, watching more Rachel Zoe, within two to three weeks.

Sincerely,
Danny Silianoff (Megan's husband)

P. S.
Clarification: While I hope to be home in two to three weeks, I don't hope to watch any more Rachel Zoe. The past few weeks have been difficult enough. Megan, however, can watch it as much as she wants. Alone.

1 COMMENT

Marc:

What great news! This is amazing! Now for a fast and speedy recovery! Meg, see if you can snag a few extra morphine bags . . . they come in handy around Christmas. We love you! So proud of you!

Wednesday, November 3, 2010
UPDATE ON MEGAN

Hi, everyone. It's Linda, Megan's mom. Wow, Megan had a really, really rough night. At midnight she woke up and felt very anxious and horrible all over, but it was not pain from the incision, which would be normal. It was something else, which made me think something was definitely wrong. She appeared extremely anxious and agitated. I called a nurse, and it was discovered she had 103 degree fever, her heart was racing, her oxygen was very low, and her hemoglobin (blood) level was dropping pretty significantly.

Within minutes there were bright lights on and all types of medical personnel in the room—doctors, nurses, lab techs, etc. Danny and Mike (her dad) were back at the hotel sleeping. Mike was supposed to fly out at 6:00 this morning, but I got a hold of him and Danny and they came immediately. Mike cancelled his flight.

They've put Megan's catheter back in, and all kinds of tests have been administered since: CAT scans, chest x-rays, urinalysis, blood work, etc. We just returned from the CAT scan and are waiting for the doctor to come in with the results. We do know she'll receive a blood transfusion here shortly.

Depending on what they find, it is possible she will be moved to ICU where she can be monitored more closely, but for now we're in her original room. We know they were looking for evidence of clots—but the doctor just now called, as I write this, and said that her lungs are definitely weakened but that is somewhat normal after surgery. Apparently there is not a clot, thank God!

For some reason they have decided she needs another CAT scan. I guess the one she had earlier wasn't clear enough or something, so we are waiting for them to come take her for that. Another day of no eating or drinking. She is so tired she literally cannot keep her eyes open.

Keep those prayers going—she has a long way to go. It is hard to watch her go "backward" but hopefully the fresh blood will help and they'll soon have things under control. Keep your comments coming as she loves when I read them to her. I'll keep you all posted as best I can. Please pray for her recovery.

Love,
Linda Halpin (Megan's mom)

1 COMMENT

Booker:
Dear Mommy, even though I miss you, I'm having fun at Aunt Kathy's house. I'm playing with my cousins, taking lots of walks, and on one particular occasion, going through the trash.

Love,
Booker

Thursday, November 4, 2010
PROOF OF LIFE

Greetings from Room 1061. It's me, Megan. I'm alive. Alive and well! More accurately, alive and high! I'm hooked up to a million different things: an IV, a catheter, some other stuff, and my most favorite thing—a morphine drip. A morphine drip that I get to control! My general philosophy on morphine is the more the merrier.

This morning has been pretty uneventful, though I did get my CAT scan results back and everything appears to be okay. The nurse keeps nagging me to get out of bed and practice walking. It's a great idea in theory. In actuality, not so much. Every time I sit up I feel like I'm gonna throw up. So for now, I'm mentally picturing myself walking around my wing of the hospital, like Olympic divers and gymnasts do. Mental visualization. I told the nurse about my plan. She told me if I didn't get up soon the only Olympics I'd be in was the "Special Olympics." I like her.

Friday, November 5, 2010
A DAY IN THE LIFE

Today has been a good day! My nurses and doctors are all happy with my progress, and I might even get to go home tomorrow. Their criteria for me doing so are based on the following:

Walking Laps
Done. I've gotten up once already and walked several laps around my particular wing. I'll do so again tonight before I go to sleep. One thing to keep in mind for any future patients out there: don't

use your IV cart as a beverage holder during the aforementioned walks. If you carefully balance your drink on your IV cart while walking, it's likely this drink will spill. It's also likely your nurse will get very pissed if this happens.

Waste Elimination

I am not going to get into this. But my body is all messed up because I had a catheter in for so long. Plus, they took it out and then had to put it back in when I took that turn for the worse. So my body is just all messed up and confused. Why am I talking about this? I'm stopping now.

Eating

Honestly, I can't believe I'm struggling with this. I love to eat. I excel at eating. I am an expert eater! I've never *not* had an appetite like this before. Where was this in college when I was packing on the freshman ~~fifteen~~ twenty-five? What's worse is that there is a Chick-fil-A in the hospital food court and I can't eat it! What a waste of good Chick-fil-A.

People who are not losing their appetite, however? My parents. My mom especially. She thinks, and I quote, the hospital food here is "amazing." Her favorite? The shrimp! The hospital shrimp! Seafood from a hospital! You see why I got so fat in college? The culinary standards in my house growing up were not exactly high.

Dress Code

The nurse keeps getting pissed at me because I refuse to wear my hospital gown and rather opt for my Victoria's Secret sweats. I asked her if MD Anderson had ever considered gowns that are less "enormous." Though she answered "no," her tone was more of a "fuck no," which I didn't appreciate.

Blow Thingy

I have this thingy that I'm supposed to blow into to strengthen my lungs. People are really into it here. I'm not convinced. Though I must say, my interest piqued when Dad offered to pay me five dollars every time I did it. I told him to make it ten dollars. I'm now getting $7.50 every time I use this contraption.

Blood Clot Leg Warmers

I'm also supposed to wear these huge leg apparatuses that prevent me from getting blood clots. They're a bitch to get on and off, though, which is why I told the nurse that "I'd prefer to not wear them and just take my chances on the clot." She laughed until she realized I was serious.

Saturday, November 6, 2010
PEACE OUT

I, Megan Silianoff, have been discharged from MD Anderson as of 11:00 a.m. today. I am still waiting on the gathering of my prescriptions and other administrative formalities. Upon their completion, however, I will vacate the premises in what I'm guessing could be record time for an MD Anderson patient. (If I sound anxious to go, it's because I am anxious to go.)

For the next few days I will be holed up in the Hyatt Hotel regaining my strength and ordering room service. Thanks to everyone for your thoughts, prayers, and positive vibes sent in my general direction. They worked!

Tuesday, November 9, 2010
MOVE OVER, HEIDI KLUM

Greetings from the Hyatt Hotel! I'm well on my way to recovery and hoping to fly home within the next few days. My follow up appointment was short and sweet. It began with the nurse asking very routine questions: name, patient number, date of birth, etc.

As the nurse asked these questions, she didn't appear to be listening to my answers. That's why I answered "crack" when she inquired about the meds I'm currently taking. Although she remained silent, she paused and gave me a look that said something along the lines of, *This one thinks she's real funny.* To which I responded with a look that said, *Yeah! Totally! I think I'm hilarious!*

Thankfully, I got along much better with the second nurse, who began taking my vitals. After taking my temperature and blood pressure, LaShonda had me stand up and walk over to the scale. She recorded my weight on my chart in kilograms and gave me the okay to push the pounds button, converting my weight to a number that meant something to me. I excitedly marveled at the number and was trying to decide if I should take a picture of it with my phone when LaShonda announced my height.

"Five feet three inches," she said routinely, writing it down on my chart.

"WHAT?!" I screamed, admittedly too dramatically, causing her to jump.

"I'm five two," I told her confidently.

"No, girl, you're five three."

"For real?" I asked excitedly.

"For real," LaShonda confirmed.

"How come everyone else has been telling me I'm five two?"

"I don't know, but you're five three."

So the jury is still out on whether LaShonda is the best nurse at MDA or the worst. Either she's the only one who can't read a height stick or the only one who can. I like to think it's the former and I have in fact grown. I have been taking a lot of vitamins lately. Vita gummy or something like that? The ones that are basically indistinguishable from gummy bears. So that could be it.

Whatever the reason, this growth spurt is super exciting. You know who else is five three? Rachel Bilson. Kim Kardashian. Sienna Miller. Tom Cruise. All my faves!

1 COMMENT

Erin:
I just slammed a ton of vita gummies. They are technically my husband's vitamins (he has trouble swallowing pills and eating anything that isn't candy), but every once in a while I need a fix. I hope it isn't bad for you to get 2700 percent of everything in one day.

Thursday, November 11, 2010
TIPS FOR YOUR NEXT MAMMOGRAM

Today I spent the entirety of my afternoon waiting for a mammogram. It's one of the last things I have to do before getting released to fly home. They know I don't have breast cancer—that's not the point of doing it. My doctor just wants to get some baseline pictures for my next mammogram, scheduled for six months from now. That way if something looks astray, she'll have pictures to compare it to.

It was terrible. Waiting, waiting, waiting. I was still waiting an hour past the time when my appointment was scheduled. I convinced myself this was no way to live. Even if I did, in fact, have breast cancer, how did I want to spend my remaining time? Cooped up in this waiting room? Or outside living life! Enjoying the sunshine! Spending time with Danny! Making it back to the hotel in time for Ellen at 4:00 p.m.! Based on this philosophy, I dramatically stood up and exited the waiting room. *Free! Free at last!* I told myself as I walked out the door—and heard the nurse call my name.

> **Nurse:** Okay, Mrs. Silianoff, please take off everything from the waist up and put it in that locker there. Please help yourself to the alcohol and—
>
> **Mrs. Silianoff:** ALCOHOL?! (Surprised)
>
> **Nurse:** Yes. Please help yourself to the alcohol and gauze prior to your procedure.
>
> **Mrs. Silianoff:** (Now seeing the array of medical supplies, including rubbing alcohol) Oh. Right.

So to all my friends who've yet to experience a mammogram, which is likely all of you, remember two things: One, be prepared to wait. Two, BYOB.

Tuesday, November 16, 2010
GREETINGS FROM CHICAGO

Home sweet home! I am writing this current, and hopefully final, post from the comforts of my condo. I can't tell you how nice it is to have the comforts of home; my dog, my bed, the 4:00

a.m. gunshots. (Totally kidding, prospective buyers of our condo! Nonprospective buyers—help! I'm scared!)

The plan for the entirety of this year is to chill at home. I'm not supposed to go up or down stairs, as this would cause scar tissue in my abdominal region, which is apparently bad. I struggle with lying around for long periods of time so I don't see this going well, but I'll do my best. Perhaps I'll pick up a hobby, like baking. Those cake pops seem to be popular right now. Though my gut tells me I'm much more likely to develop a raging addiction during my downtime. Like alcoholism. Or to my painkillers. That seems way more me.

I also want to take a quick second to thank my friend Nicole for my "bandage bling." She bought me pink and white, crystal-encrusted Band-Aids from Sephora. They are equal parts ridiculous and awesome. I have seven of them going up and down the entirety of my incision. I look like a hooker, but a high-class one for politicians and professional athletes.

Anyway, I suppose my cancer saga is winding down. At least for now and hopefully for the foreseeable future. I know 90 percent of this blog has been silly, but in all seriousness, thanks to everyone for your support. It has been overwhelming and instrumental in my remaining positive throughout the past few months. I've learned a lot about myself and those around me. Life is good.

The End.

1 COMMENT

Jo:
THE BEGINNING!

part two

Tuesday, August 9, 2011
NAGASAKI

Friends and Family,

Greetings from my new city of Houston, Texas, though I wish this salutation came under better circumstances. I have some unfortunate news, as you can probably deduct from the resurrection of this blog after nine months. In an unexpected turn of events, I now have cancer on my remaining ovary. (Sad face.) I'm having a CAT scan on Thursday to ensure the cancer hasn't spread anywhere else.

We found out last night that the cancer was back. It was a pretty big bomb. I've been calling it "Nagasaki," mostly because it makes me sound smart, being a historical reference and all.

Obviously I wasn't expecting this, so it's upsetting, but Danny and I have had twenty-four hours to process and come to terms with it.

Everyone keeps asking how I'm doing, and the answer is fine. Truly, I'm fine! Maybe it'd be more convincing if you could see my smile as I say it. Or perhaps that makes it creepy? It could go either way. The visual is there. Use if it helps.

While this is not an ideal situation, Danny and I will deal with it as we always do: with optimism, levity, humor, drugs and alcohol, and whatever else we see fit.

P. S.

To the girls I am supposed to meet in Nashville this weekend for Nicole's bachelorette party: Obviously this turn of events changes things . . . but Nashville isn't one of them! See you soon, chicas!

3 COMMENTS

Jess:
FUCK.

Jill:
Have a great time in Nashville this weekend! I'm sad I won't be able to see Nicole open the vibrator I got her, but maybe you can take a picture.

John:
I know you're fine and not worried about it—well, you probably are worried, but from what I've gathered, you try not to get too wrapped up in the things you can't control (fucking shit hole cancer) and focus on the things you can control (your attitude, your relationships, Chanel handbags). Seriously, I'm praying for you big time . . . for both things.

Wednesday, August 10, 2011
UP TO SPEED

Until yesterday, it's been nine months since I've updated this blog, so I thought before we get into the thick of cancer again, I'd bring everyone up to speed on our life in Texas. (Spoiler alert—it's hot here.)

In January 2011, we moved to Houston and leased a condo in the neighborhood known as the Medical Center. I'm pretty sure we're the only residents who aren't doctors or nurses, but we're used to being the minority. In Chicago, we were the only ones in the neighborhood who didn't speak Polish or carry a weapon.

Our condo is less than two miles from MD Anderson, so this proximity should make my frequent trips to the hospital quite convenient. Due to my bad directional sense, however, I've yet to reach the hospital without getting significantly lost, and therefore travel time is comparable to what it would be coming from Chicago.

Within weeks of moving, I found a full-time job recruiting at a staffing firm. Though this firm had many different recruiting divisions, I was recruiting exclusively within its medical arm. I thought my background in recruiting paired with my recently acquired patient experience would make me a perfect fit for the role. I was right. Without bragging, I must say it was pretty easy for me to jump in. I placed a few people within just a week or so. The only thing I ended up being wrong about was my desire to work. Turns out, I didn't want to. Who knew? I quit three weeks into the job and have spent the majority of my days snacking, watching "The View," and trying to teach Booker tricks.

Danny, no longer working from home, continues to work in electronic discovery. He likes having an office to go to every day and is very happy with the opportunities moving here has offered him professionally. When I pressed him for a downside of his new job, he only mentioned that he "wishes his wife would stop prank calling throughout the day."

After just two months of living in Texas, Danny took me to my first rodeo at Reliant Stadium. Though skeptical of rodeos, as I previously mentioned, I must say that I thoroughly enjoyed the event. My rodeo highlights consisted of riding a camel, eating a fried snickers bar, drinking Bud Light, petting a goat, and purchasing a pair of chaps that said *Houston Rodeo 2011*. Danny protested my purchase, his argument being "When are you ever going to wear those?" The answer being my LinkedIn profile picture and two times to the airport when retrieving him from business trips.

I have to say though, overall, we love Houston: the weather, our spacious condo, the abundance of Chick-fil-As, and just the comfort of knowing I'm so close to my doctors should an issue ever arise. (Like now, for example.)

The downside of Texas, of course, is that we're so far from our friends and my family, and that's definitely hard. We are gradually making friends, though. Danny has a buddy, Mark, with whom he grew up in Lufkin, Texas. Mark is living in the Houston suburbs, and we've been hanging with him and his wife, Michele, who I love. I especially love her accent, which she honed growing up in East Texas. Michele says things like "that guy wouldn't say shit even if his mouth was full of it," which I get a huge kick out of. I actually tried to incorporate this saying into a conversation with my neighbors recently, but I messed it up and ended up saying something along the lines of "Danny has shit in his mouth." It was awkward. Especially for Danny.

We've also been hanging with the CFO of Danny's company and his wife. Their names are Jeremy and Jill, and they too are really cool. Jill is a spitting image of the *Parenthood* actress Erika Christensen, but she hates it when I say that, though I'm not sure why. Maybe because Erika is known to be a scientologist? Scientologists always get a bad rap.

Jeremy, like Danny, is a hunter, and the two bond significantly over this hobby. Unlike Danny, however, Jeremy has been known to shoot feral cats in his neighborhood. Apparently that's a thing here in Texas. Feral cats. They're everywhere. Initially I didn't have a strong grasp on the definition of feral, which is why I got so upset at dinner a few weeks ago when Jeremy told us he shot them. I misunderstood "feral" to be the last name of Jeremy and Jill's neighbors and was shocked to hear Jeremy had committed such a malicious act. I quickly excused myself from the table until

Danny realized I was confused and intervened with another glass of pinot noir and a quick vocabulary lesson.

Last, and certainly not least, I should mention that Danny and I are in the process of making Booker a big brother. (Gasp!) I am not preggo, clearly, but it is equally exciting: we're adopting! We started navigating this process almost immediately after moving to Houston, and for those of you who know nothing about adoption, the most important thing to know is that the process is a real bitch.

In March of this year we got off to a very quick but rough start with an agency that we'll call BSA (acronym for Bull Shit Agency). Danny and I disclosed to BSA from the get-go that I had a medical history of cancer, and they were fine with it. They were supposed to be a "cancer friendly" agency, which is why we choose them in the first place.

In attempt to make a long story short, I will say that six months into working with BSA they told us they wouldn't work with us because, well, *I had a medical history of cancer*. Uh, no shit! It was infuriating. This was, of course, after we had invested over a grand into their agency by attending their weekend orientation, paying various application fees, etc.

They drew it out too. At first it was "they need a letter stating that I had an average life span despite the cancer." Then it was "a written guarantee from my doctor that the cancer wouldn't return." Doctor Bear was actually super helpful and was jumping through all of their hoops with us. But of course she couldn't guarantee that my cancer would never return. Nobody can. It's a ridiculous thing to ask for in the first place.

Danny and I handled the situation with the utmost class, if I do say so myself. Though it was difficult, I refrained from sending BSA any nasty e-mails, phone calls, anthrax packages, etc.

I wasn't mad that they chose not to work with us because of my cancer—that's fair and it's their prerogative. Millions of agencies won't work with us because of that. I was pissed because they had jerked us around and wasted our time.

The good news is we've since licked our wounds and found another agency in Austin that appears to be much more forthcoming. Danny and I could be parents in the relatively near future! It could be tomorrow, it could be two years from now. It's just a matter of getting that call that a birthmother wants to meet us. Needless to say this is a very exciting but crazy situation.

Thursday, August 11, 2011
DR. ALEX

Since we moved to Houston, I've been going to MDA every three months for ultrasounds to make sure my ovarian area looks legit. Even last week, when I thought I was perfectly healthy, I was somewhat eager for the appointment because I would be meeting my new doctor. Sadly, Dr. Bear took a position at the MD Anderson in Arizona and no longer sees patients in Houston. It's a bummer because I really liked and trusted her. Plus, I think she was world-renowned in the gynecologic world. It's less sexy than the celeb world, but probably better in the context of my situation.

My appointment sheet read that I had been assigned to Dr. Alex. Assuming Dr. Alex was a man, I was surprised when a cute little Indian girl donned in Tory Burch flats walked in my room. This was my doctor? Come on! She could be my friend, sure, especially if she let me borrow her shoes, but no way was she old enough to be my doctor!

I must say, however, Dr. Alex disarmed me of any concern quickly. I liked her right away. She was soft spoken, wasn't awkward when navigating small talk, and everything that came out of her mouth seemed fair and logical. Plus, I Googled her. In lieu of drunken Facebook pictures I found her study on "novel therapeutic drug targets for treatment of ovarian cancer." So I'm sure she's legit.

My ultrasound at this appointment, however, showed that I had something on my ovary. While this is less than ideal, it's not cause for panic. The "something" easily could have been a random follicle temporarily stationed on my ovary, especially given where I was in my menstrual cycle. That's what Dr. Alex explained to me anyway. She did say that she felt "fullness" when administering my internal exam, but even that she didn't seem overly concerned about. She was waiting for the results of my CA-125, which would give her more info, and told me she'd call me upon receiving them. I went home cautiously optimistic.

Dr. Alex called around fiveish to let me know my CA-125 was elevated, which she never came out and said was bad, but she didn't need to. I could tell from her tone. She explained that the CA-125 test is indicative of tumors. So the higher the results of the test, the higher the chance you have a tumor. My ultrasound paired with the fullness paired with an elevated CA-125 test was reason to panic. The cancer was back. Fuck!

Dr. Alex calmly told me she was scheduling a CAT scan so we could make sure the cancer was contained to the same stomach/ovarian area. After that, she'd have me come back in and we'd decide where to go from there. "Okay," I told her and then hung up my phone and set it down on my desk.

Danny was out in the living room. "It's back," I said as tears streamed down my face, and he stared at me blankly.

"Let's go for a walk," I told him. "I want to walk."

So we did. We put Booker on his leash and walked for a mile, maybe two, just talking it out. I told him I didn't want to tell my parents until the next day in hopes of giving them twelve more hours of serenity. He agreed. I also told him I wanted to take a trip to Vietnam because "life is short and we should just go because things are about to get crazy and this might be our last chance." That was a harder sell.

Danny's thoughts were probably a little more typical. He was pissed. He thought the whole thing was bullshit and that we'd been through enough. He was upset and angry that we had to do a round two.

When we got back home, I still had too much adrenaline rushing through my body to be able sit down on the couch. I grabbed my iPod, turned on some Rihanna, and went for a run through Hermann Park. The same park that separates my condo from MD Anderson. *I'll be fine,* I thought. *I'm running, for God's sake, how sick can I possibly be if I'm running like this?*

I came home feeling better: positive, physically (and emotionally) drained, and ready for dinner. I could tell Danny was feeling better too. We had processed. The worst part, or at least that part, was over. So now it's your turn, friends. Feel better about this! This isn't my first rodeo; I'll be fine, I promise! Especially if I can make that Vietnam trip happen.

Friday, August 12, 2011
CAT SCAN

I was in a good mood this morning as I entered the hospital, upbeat even. I think it's because I've accepted that I'm having surgery again, and with acceptance comes tranquility. Or maybe it was my outfit. I really liked my outfit. I was wearing a white T-shirt that said *Brooklyn* on it; I'd tracked it down online after seeing Beyoncé wear it in US Weekly! I paired the shirt with gray skinny jeans and black booties, my hair was all waved out, and I put on bright red lipstick—just as Beyoncé had styled it. The lips were probably overboard given the day I had in store, but whatever, I was feeling upbeat.

I checked into the CAT scan area and got my barium. Do you guys know what barium is? It's a thick liquid you drink that makes your insides light up so that they're easily visible on a CAT scan. By the way, breaking news on barium! They have new flavors now: apple and coconut! Not together. They have apple. They also have coconut. But apple/coconut would probably be good too.

I was drinking my barium and plopped down on a bench next to a nice elderly lady who was also drinking barium. We checked out each other's flavors and swapped stories as cancer patients tend to do.

Sweet Old Lady: Is that apple good?

Me: It's super good! Best barium I've had yet.

Sweet Old Lady: Oh. I just drink banana.

Me: Can't go wrong with banana. So what're you in here for?

Sweet Old Lady: I come every six weeks for chemo.

Me: You're doing chemo? But you have your hair!

Sweet Old Lady: Barely. It's very thin. My daughter-in-law bought me a wig and keeps trying to make me wear it.

Me: You don't need a wig. Tell your daughter-in-law to back off! (Said with emphasis)

Random Person: (Interrupting) Hey, Mom. They are ready for you.

Sweet Old Lady: This is my daughter-in-law.

Me: Oh. Hey!

(Awkwardness ensues.)

My CAT scan, unfortunately, also had awkward undertones. I felt like my thirty-something, Indian, male radiologist was flirting with me. Not all "Hey baby, what you doing later," but he knew I lived in Houston and we shared some witty banter regarding our esteemed city. He told me he liked my pink, crystal-covered iPhone case. He went on to say that if he had the same one, he'd have to move to Houston's Montrose neighborhood because it's where the gays live. I don't know if that conversation counts as witty. Perhaps that's more racist? Stereotypical? Regardless, it was hard to transition from this conversation to his next line: "Okay Mrs. Silianoff, I'm going to put tubes in your butt now." It's just so embarrassing.

"Flirting" isn't even the right word. I think the problem is that often a lot of the medical professionals I encounter at MDA are surprised by my age. Surely there must be thousands of patients in their twenties. Early thirties even. But I've never seen one. Not one! Isn't that crazy?

Don't get me wrong, the connecting is nice, and I appreciate everyone being what feels like extra nice to me, but when they want to transition from the "connecting" portion of the visit to me, for example, showing them my boobs, it's just weird. Weirder than it would be had we not just bonded over our hatred of cilantro. Does that make sense?

Monday, August 15, 2011
CAT SCAN RESULTS

It's funny. All weekend I haven't been too worried about my results, all things considered. But the minute I got out of bed today, I felt the nerves. The thought of breakfast was unappetizing. I was ready to get the show on the road.

We arrived at the hospital with just a few minutes to spare prior to my appointment. I wanted to stop and get coffee from the hospital café, but I also didn't want to be late. Had I known I had time to not only get coffee but cultivate the beans myself, I would have slowed down and relaxed while pouring myself a cup of Starbucks.

Coffee in hand, I checked in with the front desk coordinator of the GYN floor. Before I could even say anything, she said, all chipper, "Good morning, Ms. Silianoff!"

"Good morning!" I said back, surprised and excited that she knew who I was. Though in hindsight, I realize being recognized at a hospital isn't a good thing. It means you are there too damn often. (Same goes with bars.)

Then the waiting began. Waiting, waiting, waiting. Danny and I waited half an hour and didn't think much of it. We expect to wait. But when we hit the hour mark I was pissed.

The nurse finally invited us back behind the closed doors and took my vitals. She asked the usual stuff: current medications, if I was in pain, had I fallen recently. (I actually had fallen recently. But I'm pretty sure it wasn't cancer-related. Just drunk. I decided not to share.)

The nurses then escorted Danny and me into the conference room, where we waited another hour for the doctor. That clocked us in at two hours of total wait time! Bullshit, right? I mean, it would be one thing if I were just waiting to have a general exam or something. But waiting two hours to find out if my cancer had spread? That's just cold. Danny and I tried to make the best of it by staying busy with countless games of tic-tac-toe and hangman. (Oh, who won hangman? I did. With the words *xerox* and *testicle*.)

At last the door opened and in walked Dr. Alex. She apologized for keeping us waiting, though with just one look at her, I had forgotten we had. Her cute little face represented my fate and I wanted to know what that was. Out with it already.

She tried showing me the images of my CAT scan on her computer. Tried and failed. I'm sure some patients love that—very visual-learner-type people. I wasn't interested though. I didn't need any visual, tangible proof to believe what she was about to tell me. I believed her. What I needed from her was to get to the bottom line as soon as possible. Death? Chemo? Had it spread? What were we looking at here? Bottom line it.

The cancer hasn't spread. Yay! I mean, it's not 100 percent sure, but as far as she can tell, it's contained to my ovary. We scheduled surgery for the 25th of this month and that was pretty much it. Much like my previous surgery, Dr. Alex will decide the course of action while I'm on the table. Since this is my only ovary, she'll be as conservative as possible—only removing the entire ovary if it's too cancer ridden to save.

2 COMMENTS

Kristen:
How does Danny not know by now that *xerox* is your go-to word for hangman?

Megan replied:
The key is the *x*. No one ever guesses *x*.

Thursday, August 18, 2011
DRAMA

We had a little drama last night in the Silianoff household. It started off as a very normal evening. Danny made fish tacos and we settled in to some "Top Chef." I went to bed not feeling stellar, but I'd had a glass of wine with dinner and attributed it to that. Mistake. I woke up a little after midnight in agony. Sheer agony, I tell you! Without getting too intimate, I felt like I had to pee but I couldn't. Nothing would come out.

I looked at myself in the mirror and immediately knew it wasn't good. I was white. Too white. Scary white. This probably had something to do with why I collapsed on the ground moments later. What happened after that was sort of a blur. I felt myself falling deeper and deeper into the shower bathmat. I do remember calling for Danny and us trying to decide if we should call an ambulance. We needed to go to the ER—that was obvious. But we were trying to decide if I could sit up long enough for Danny to carry me to the car. I couldn't. Danny called 911.

I remember Danny yelling at me to stay awake while we waited for the ambulance. "MEGAN! MEGAN! STAY AWAKE SWEETIE! MEGAN, YOU HAVE TO STAY AWAKE! LOOK AT ME! MEGAN!" Danny never calls me "Megan." I'm "Baby" or "Honey" or whatever. Using my proper name like that sounded foreign and was a telltale sign that he was scared. That made me that much more scared.

With my eyes closed, I asked Danny to pour water on my head. I don't really remember being hot, but I must have instinctually known what my body wanted. He discounted my plea at first because it's kind of a weird request. But after I started screaming at him, "JUST DO IT! DO IT NOW! DO IT!" he felt more compelled.

I felt instant relief as he dumped a massive cup of lukewarm water on my head. The more water he poured, the better I felt. I assume this meant I had some sort of fever and the water helped break it? I don't know. I just know it felt good.

Soon I heard the paramedics' male voices as they stomped up the stairs to our master bathroom, where I was still lying on the floor. Even in my agony, I could see that the EMT who kneeled down next to me was hot. Smoking hot. While this is not necessarily a bad thing, it's not what I was looking for, given the situation. Not only did I look like I'd just been through some sort of bizarre baptism with my soaking wet head, I was also naked from the waist down. The last thing I wanted was to be in the presence of some hot-ass dude.

The hot paramedic took my vitals as Danny debriefed him on my situation: cancer, imminent surgery, blah, blah, blah. Obviously I wanted to go the MD Anderson ER, but these paramedics didn't have a contract with my hospital. They weren't allowed to take me there based on the ambulance bureaucracy rules. Instead, they carried me to Danny's Tahoe and placed me in the backseat.

Just when I thought the night couldn't get any more embarrassing, it got more embarrassing. The route from our master bathroom to Danny's Tahoe involved going through my kitchen, which would have been an insignificant detail on any other night. But as it just so happened, on this particular night, my kitchen was storing a life-size cutout of a naked man.

You see, I was appointed (by myself) head of the "game committee" for this weekend's bachelorette party in Nashville. As head of this committee I created a very tasteful, though admittedly graphic, version of the classic game "Pin the Tail on the Donkey." My version is called "Pin the Tail on Peter." Instead of pinning tails on Peter, we pin penises!

Obviously the demographic for my game is not hot male EMTs in their twenties. This is why, judging by the look on Hot Paramedic's face, he wasn't a fan. He looked horrified. But like I said—not the right demographic. I have complete confidence my friends will love it.

The drama really ends there. We spent all night in the ER doing lots of waiting. I, at least, got to be in a bed, as opposed to my poor husband, who sat in his token chair. The ER doc diagnosed me as having a "rip-roaring" bladder infection and prescribed me something for it. He couldn't diagnose nor explain the fainting part of my story. He thought maybe I jumped out of bed too fast. I didn't know if that was necessarily it, but went with it because I just wanted to get the hell out of there. Most importantly, he thinks I'll be fine for my surgery next week as long as I diligently take the antibiotic he prescribed.

Monday, August 22, 2011
NASHVILLE

Home sweet home. I'm back from Nashville, y'all! It was a good time had by all! It was so good to catch up with all my college compadres, and considering how crazy they are, I'm proud of the PG behavior I maintained all weekend. I didn't drink but one glass of celebratory champagne and I went back to the hotel both nights at 10:00 p.m. Despite this, I was still pretty exhausted upon boarding my flight home. This is precisely why I had no interest in chatting up my Southwest seatmate, who introduced himself to me as Dale from Fort Worth, Texas. I could immediately tell this guy was going to be a Chatty Cathy and really wanted us to get to know one another.

Dale: I was in Nashville on business. I'm a lubricant salesman.

Me: Ha! Lubricant you say?

Dale: Indeed.

Me: So tell me, Dale, how's the lube business these days?

Dale: It's quite good.

Me: Ha! Really? Too bad I didn't meet you on the way *to* Nashville. I would have bought some from you. I was there for a bachelorette party!

Dale: How do you mean?

Me: You know, bachelorette parties. You give the bride gag gifts!

Dale: I beg your pardon?

Me: Lube! Ha!

Then Dale got kinda quiet for the rest of our flight, which was fine by me. It wasn't until I told this story to Danny that I learned about industrial lubricant and that this is probably what Dale sells as opposed to having a briefcase full of KY jelly like I had envisioned. Still, though, at the end of the day, the guy sells lube.

Tuesday, August 23, 2011
NEXT OF KIN

Cigna called to verify my insurance today. Overall, it didn't go well. Let's just say the lady and I got off to a rough start. I thought she was saying "Mexican," but she was really saying "next of kin." I can't be the only person this has ever happened to. Right? Right, guys?

Receptionist: Please confirm your full name, ma'am.

Me: Megan Silianoff.

Receptionist: And your date of birth, ma'am?

Me: November 17, 1981.

Receptionist: Is your address still 455 Camden Road, ma'am?

Me: It is.

Receptionist: And your next of kin, ma'am?

Me: No. I'm white.

Receptionist: Excuse me?

Me: I'm white. Like, Caucasian, you know?

Receptionist: I'm saying next of kin, ma'am!

Me: Oh! Ha! Wait . . . what's that?

Wednesday, August 24, 2011
DO OR DIE

So tomorrow's the big day. Do or die time, though that's probably not the best idiom for this situation.

I'm obviously nervous. Though, this being the third time around, I have different worries than I've had previously. I remember my first surgery in Chicago: being so scared that they wouldn't give me enough anesthesia and I'd wake up in the middle of the surgery, able to feel everything. That seems silly now.

I guess "worried" isn't even the right word for what I'm feeling. More anxious. Anxious and eager to find out what type of cancer I have. Is it LMP again? Or just your run-of-the-mill ovarian cancer?

I'm not scared, though. I know that I'm in good hands. I completely trust Dr. Alex and her team. I also know that, based on my CAT scan, the cancer is isolated to my ovary, meaning that it hasn't spread. So how bad can the outcome possibly be?

Lastly and most importantly, I know that no matter what goes down, there is nothing I can do about it. My fate is sealed, and that gives me a sense of peace as well. But I'm still anxious. Anxious that tomorrow at this time I could be down an ovary. Or in menopause. Or chemo bound. I really don't want to do chemo.

Perhaps the reason I'm keeping it together is that I haven't had time to think about it today. My pre-op appointments took about three times longer than I anticipated. Waiting to see Dr. Alex. Waiting to see Dr. Alex's nurse. Waiting to see the anesthesiologist. All the unanticipated waiting meant I didn't get home until almost five.

Originally I had wanted to have an amazing "last meal" today. Perhaps go out for Indian food or pizza with Danny. Starting tomorrow I won't have an appetite for at least a week as my pain pills will diminish it completely. But because I was at the hospital for so long and I need to start my prep by 5:00, we didn't have time. I settled for some scrambled eggs and cantaloupe—the only stuff we had in the fridge.

Do you guys know what I mean when I say "my prep?" The most definitive quality about the prepping process is that it blows. It's the worst part of the entire surgery process for sure. From what I gather, it's the same thing people have to do prior to a colonoscopy. The prep is a thick, clear, flavored liquid that you have to drink. Tonight's flavor was orange, which was especially awful due to a specific night I had in college involving orange Bacardi.

The prep always, without fail, makes me gag the minute it hits my tongue, which is problematic when you have to drink two gallons of it. It's so much worse than the barium. Barium is like champagne compared to this prep drink. The point of drinking it, of course, is to clean you out by making you go to the bathroom. This makes your body safer to operate on. But it's never once done that to me. Not for my previous surgeries or tonight. Instead I just vomit.

In fact, just an hour ago I was in my kitchen with my mom (who's down with my dad for the surgery) trying to finish off the last of my second gallon. I told her if I took one more sip, I'd puke. I could tell she thought I was being dramatic. So I took one more sip and puked. The satisfaction of being right made throwing up a little more enjoyable.

I guess I should try to get some sleep. My alarm is set for 5:00 a.m. as we have to be at the hospital by 6:00 a.m.

4 COMMENTS

Aunt Debbie:
Don't forget your princess sweatshirt that I bought you. They need to know who you are!

Megan replied:
No worries, Aunt Debs! I have the sweatshirt packed, but my princess status usually becomes apparent quickly, with or without the sweatshirt.

Kate:
Your man Jay-Z once said, "I keep it fresher than the next bitch, no need for you to ever sweat the next bitch." In this case the "next bitch" is referring to tomorrow's surgery. And by not sweating it, I think he means you will get through it no prob.

Megan replied:
HOV.

Thursday, August 25, 2011
OUT OF SURGERY

Hi everyone, this is Megan's aunt, Debbie. I just got off the phone with Linda (Megan's mom) and wanted to update everyone accordingly. Linda called around 12:40 p.m. and told me the following:

Around 10:00 a.m., mid-surgery, they took some of Megan's ovarian tissue to the lab. They were able to save some of Megan's ovary and ovarian tissue. Hopefully enough to prevent menopause, but it doesn't sound like it's for sure. She apparently has so much scar tissue from her previous surgeries that it took forever to actually get the doctors' retraction instruments in there and do what they needed to do.

There was more cancer on the ovary than expected, but it all appears to be LMP—not invasive cancer! It's not official until the pathology results are back next week, but initially it is good news.

Megan got an epidural this time around as well as general anesthesia, so the doctor thinks this will help with her getting up and moving around. If all goes well with recovery, she may be in the hospital only three days.

Again, if the pathology comes back as invasive cancer, she'll need chemo. But as it looks now it's the LMP she had previously.

Megan is in recovery now. I think Linda needs a bed next to her with some Ambien. She sounded so tired. She'll let us know when they have been assigned a room.

Sincerely,
Debbie Vandenberg (Megan's aunt)

Sunday, August 28, 2011
WEEKEND UPDATE

I'd like to tell you something about epidurals. They're awesome. I feel like epidurals are often part of the birthing process but get overshadowed because of the baby. Yes, babies are great, *obviously*. But so are epidurals! I don't know why I've never received an epidural in my previous surgeries. I asked my anesthesiologist (seriously, you guys should have seen that word before my spell check intervened) and she said that some surgeons just don't like to give them. But my anesthesiologist suggested it to Dr. Alex and she was down. Just another reason I like her so much.

Other exciting hospital updates? Booker visisted yesterday! Due to strict MD Anderson policy, he couldn't come up to my room, but Danny brought him to the hospital entrance and I stepped outside to see him. It was awesome! It would have been more awesome if the guy next to us hadn't been eating a hot dog and completely preoccuping Booker's attention during our visit. But good stuff nonetheless.

Next up on the agenda is a blood tranfusion, which sounds scary (or exciting for all you Twilight fans! Team Edward!), but it just means that I'll be hooked up to a bag of blood that goes into my body. Dr. Alex had mentioned to me after surgery that I was anemic, but that was to be expected as I'd been open on the table for over four hours. If possible, she preferred for me to try to recover on my own, without the transfusion.

Until this afternoon, it looked like that wouldn't be a problem, but I'm actually starting to feel worse, not better. I'm too faint and nauseous to get out of bed, and if I don't get out of bed, I can't go home. From what I'm told by the attending doctors (Dr. Alex went home for the weekend), the transfusion works instantly—it's like being hungry and then eating food.

They assure me it's possible that I could still can go home tonight. I hope so! I'm going to have to be significantly better at receiving blood than giving it. I can't help thinking back to high school when my friend Stacie and I decided to participate in the blood drive because it got you out of class. I got so lightheaded and nauseous that I vomited in my locker, which was not ideal. Though the vomiting resulted in more missed class, which was ideal.

And that, y'all, has been your "Weekend Update" from the hospital. I think we can all agree that it failed in comparison to the SNL version, but considering I'm high on morphine and super nauseated, I think it was above subpar.

2 COMMENTS

Stacie:
I thought we did the blood drive for the cookies. Remember how you got those warm Otis Spunkmeyer cookies when you were done? I remember being that being the big motivator.

Megan replied:
You're right. Cookies played a crucial role in our decision-making process, as they do in most decisions I make to this day.

Tuesday, August 30, 2011
HOME SWEET HOME

I have to tell you. Living five minutes from the hospital is really awesome. It's so great to be in my own bed! The Hyatt I stayed in after my last surgery was nice too. It had a Starbucks and that was pretty fantastic. I could definitely go for a Chai Tea Latte right now. But to be home, in my own bed, is so much better. And being in bed is precisely what I've been doing. My parents have gone home to Milwaukee. Danny has gone back to work. Booker is right here, lying next to me. Life is good! Especially because the pathology is back from my surgery and it was all LMP, meaning no chemo!

The only thing I could possibly complain about is my stupid DVR. Apparently there is something called HBO and something else called HBO Latino. I recorded Entourage on the latter, meaning all my episodes are in Spanish. I tried watching anyway. I was a Spanish major in college, after all. Plus, I wanted to see if they'd call Turtle *Tortuga* (my favorite Spanish word), which they totally did. I chuckled every time they did that. It reminded me of the Spanish name I choose for myself in high school: Margarita. I chuckled every time I heard that as well, which is why my teacher made me change it.

In case it's not completely evident, things are getting back to normal around here.

Sunday, September 4, 2011
HIVES

Danny and I went to Austin this weekend to see his mom. I'm not quite ready to resume life at my usual pace, but I was going stir-crazy at home. Danny's mom, Jessie, lives just three hours away in Austin and her house always is so warm and inviting— the perfect place for me to chill and recover with some fresh scenery.

Jessie is not the typical mother-in-law. From what I gather, mother-in-laws tend to be passive aggressive, hard to please, and difficult. Jessie, however, is nothing of the sort. She's sweet, fun, and has lived a hell of a life! When Jessie was just eighteen, she married an artist and together they left Pontiac, Michigan, for Los Angeles. He worked as an artist while she waitressed at the Copper Skillet Coffee Shop, a diner off of Hollywood Boulevard, where her regulars included the Monkees, the Osmonds, and the Righteous Brothers.

Unfortunately Jessie's marriage didn't turn out the way she'd hoped as her husband wasn't bringing home anything to support the four kids they had. It became so bad and desperate that Jessie ended up filing for divorce, which was a huge deal because it was 1972—divorce wasn't commonplace back then like it is today.

Jessie and her four kids eventually moved to Chicago and she started waitressing at the Hyatt Hotel and denying the advances of a short but cute little golf pro who would come to the restaurant. "Honey, you want nothing to do with me. I have four kids," she'd tell him. But of course he wanted something to do with her because—what I've yet to mention—Jessie was, and still is, gorgeous and glamorous. Even now, at seventy-five years old, she wears lashes every day—regardless of whether she's leaving the house or not.

Things with the golf pro moved quickly. The first thing he ever bought Jessie was a Clark bar and, shortly after that, a wedding ring. Jessie and the golf pro went on to have two kids—the first of whom was Danny. Danny was symbolic of a new beginning for Jessie—everything was going to be easier, happier, and fun! I can relate to that, as that's precisely the way I felt when I met him. Maybe that's one of the reasons Jessie and I get along so well. We both love Danny, but not in that competitive manner that sometimes happens with mothers and daughters-in-laws.

Anyway, this weekend at Jessie's was perfect. We wore pajamas exclusively, minus the one time we went out to have dinner at "the club," not be confused with "da club," which is something entirely different. There was a Golden Girls marathon, mass consumption of BLT sandwiches, and a daily happy hour that commenced at 4:00 sharp. (Wine for them, pain pill for me!)

There was only one setback that occurred over the weekend. A major setback, actually, in that I have hives. So many hives! They really came to full fruition Sunday evening. As Danny and his mom were calling it a night, mine was just beginning. I didn't sleep a wink, as my hives were developing at a rapid pace. Knowing that there wasn't much I could do about it until the morning, I made the best of the situation by watching Selena Gomez's *True Hollywood Story* on E! (Two thumbs up, by the way.) I also took half a package of Benadryl. That's considerably more than the package recommends—the directions seemed partial to a single capsule, but, trust me, that would have been like using an umbrella during Hurricane Katrina.

Why do I have hives? No idea! I've never had them before in my life, so it's got to be related to the surgery in some capacity. Maybe it's an allergic reaction of some sort? Or maybe it's Austin? In addition to its reputation for "being weird," Austin apparently has a lot of Mountain Cedar pollen. According to my Internet research, Mountain Cedar gives people terrible allergies. Whatever the reason may be, it's not good. I have an appointment with an allergy doctor tomorrow, so until then I'll be incorporating holistic home remedies via Web MD and other random medical sites I can find.

Tuesday, September 6, 2011
DR. CARTER

I like my new allergy doctor. He's a smooth cat. He fist bumps. He fist bumped me on his way out of the examination room, which I think should be the new standard for anyone who practices medicine. Any of you doctors reading this, write that down. Patients like fist bumps.

Dr. Carter doesn't know why I have hives, despite receiving my lengthy medical history. He thinks my surgery definitely played a part in their occurrence, but to what extent he does not know. Maybe it was the blood transfusion? Maybe it's the change in my hormones? Maybe my immune system is too compromised to fight off stuff like it normally does? Most likely all those things played a part. Regardless, my "allergy trigger," as Dr. Carter calls it, has been set off, and once it's off all you can do is compensate with medicine. Guess what medicine Dr. Carter has prescribed? Steroids! Ha!

Until today, my only knowledge of steroids came from a documentary of José Canseco. A few minutes into this documentary I learned that things weren't going to end well for Mr. Canseco, so I was skeptical of Dr. Carter's plan. Especially when I learned the specifics.

> **Dr. Carter:** I'm going to get you on a steroid, Megan.
> **Me:** Steroids? Really?
> **Dr. Carter:** Yes.
> **Me:** Huh. Now is that a pill or will I shoot it up?
> **Dr. Carter:** *You* won't be shooting anything. We'll give it to you intravenously.
> **Me:** Really? Okay. Now, is this going to make me all muscle-y like Jessica Biel or something?

Dr. Carter: Who's Jessica Biel? Is that your oncologist?

Me: No! Jessica Biel! You don't know who Jessica Biel is?

Dr. Carter: Oh. I actually do. I guess I'm struggling to follow this conversation despite being in it. No, the steroid won't make you "muscle-y." You're thinking of a completely different type of steroid.

Me: Oh. Well, let's do it then.

Dr. Carter: My nurse will actually be the one to do it here in a minute. Do you have any more questions before I leave?

Me: No. I think I'm good.

Dr. Carter: Okay then. I've enjoyed meeting you, Megan. Best of luck to you!

(Cue fist bump.)

Despite having the steroid shot, I still have a few hives. They're persistent little bastards. Dr. Carter had to prescribe an additional oral steroid, along with some other stuff, to help keep them at bay. Between the 'roids and my cancer medicines, I'm on like six different things. My pharmacist, Bruce at CVS, seemed genuinely impressed and excited by this when I went to gather my winnings. Pharmacists don't work on commission, do they? That would explain his extreme enthusiasm. Regardless, his sentiment was appreciated. It's not everyday someone is so interested in antihistamines. Shout out to you, Pharmacist Bruce!

Tuesday, September 13, 2011
MEDICAL EMERGENCY-ISH

There was another medical emergency in my house. Not me. Or Danny. But poor little Booker. I found a small but noticeable cyst on Booker's chest. Frantic, I called the vet and made an immediate appointment.

> **Vet:** So what brings you here today?
> **Me:** Booker has a cyst that I just noticed and wanted you to take a look at. (I showed her said cyst)
> **Vet:** That?! (Surprised) That's his nipple!
> **Me:** Excuse me?
> **Vet:** That's just his nipple. Do you see the other ones all up and down his belly?
> **Me:** I do now.
> **Vet:** Yeah. So anything else I can do for you today?
> **Me:** I guess not. I feel foolish.
> **Vet:** Well . . . you should.

She didn't say that. Although I'm sure she wanted to. Instead, she just charged me forty dollars for the visit. In my defense, Booker has a big-ass nipple.

Wednesday, September 21, 2011
PICKING MY COLOR

Yesterday I got my nails done at my usual spot with my usual girl. Unusually, my manicurist was wearing a MD Anderson Cancer Center T-shirt. These are pretty common in Houston, especially in the Medical Center area where I live. It's a HUGE hospital and I always assume that people sporting these shirts either work at MDA or are patients there.

Because I know my manicurist is a manicurist, I deduced that she was a patient. Extremely discreetly, I winked it at her and whispered, "I'm a patient there too." In my mind, I imagined that she'd recently been diagnosed and assumed my comment would be encouraging. What I did not picture was what actually happened.

Manicurist: You patient where? (She bellowed loudly in her thick Asian accent)
Me: (Whispering and embarrassed) Oh, uh . . . MD Anderson. Like your T-shirt says. (I pointed to her shirt)
Manicurist: You patient? You cancer?
Me: (Still whispering, hoping to encourage her to do so as well) Uh. Yeah.
Manicurist: No. I don't go there. You poor girl. Have cancer. You okay? You die?
Me: No, I don't die . . .

Just when I thought it couldn't get worse, it got worse; she started tearing up. She ceased filing my nails, got out of her seat, and hugged me as the rest of the salon stared.

Me: Uh, can I pick my color now? I'm gonna go ahead and pick my color.

I got up and took even longer than usual to inspect the hundreds of OPI polish bottles laid out before me. I ended up selecting a really dark purple. I turned the bottle over to see the name of the polish, as OPI always names their colors something fun. "Tomorrow Never Dies" it said in clear print. *Are you kidding me?* I said to myself and put it back to choose something else.

Friday, September 23, 2011
ADOPTION PRESCREEN

Today Danny and I got an e-mail from Reagan, our caseworker at the adoption agency, informing us about a birthmother she thought we might be interested in. This is the second time we've been e-mailed like this—the first one not materializing into any activity.

Perhaps I should back up before I go any further and give you little crash course on adoption. Before even being put on "the list" and becoming an official family-in-waiting, like Danny and I are, you have to jump through a million and one hoops. Paperwork, paperwork, paperwork is the bulk of it. Danny called the adoption process his "part-time job."

In addition to completing the formal adoption application (that contains an essay section!), you have to pull together an extensive list of supplemental forms: physicians' reports, criminal history background checks (that we had to go to the police department for! WTF!), marriage verification, three letters of reference, employment verifications, past tax returns, a urine sample, insurance statements, copies of driver licenses, and way more, but I'll spare you. Also I was kidding about the urine sample, but I wouldn't be surprised.

There's also a mandatory weekend orientation hosted by the agency. You also have to hire a social worker to come to your house, three separate times, to interview you and ensure your home is indeed safe for a bambino.

Anyway, somewhere throughout this process, you tell the agency what you're willing to accept and not accept in terms of what they call "a case" when a baby is concerned. For example, are Danny and I willing to accept a baby who's been exposed to alcohol? If so, how much exposure? A drink a week is not too concerning. But what if it's three drinks a week? Are we willing to pass on a baby because of that?

Then there are drugs. Are we willing to take a baby that's been exposed to drugs?

If so, what drugs?

What about cigarettes? Are we open to a baby who's been subjected to cigarette smoke for nine months?

What if the birthmother has depression?

What about more serious mental illnesses, like bipolar disorder?

What race of baby are we willing to accept?

Are we open to a Hispanic baby?

What about a black baby?

What about a half-black, half-Hispanic baby?

What are we open to in terms of age?

Should we limit ourselves to newborns?

Are we open to a six-month-old?

What about a two-year-old?

And then, *at last,* your brain explodes!

As you can imagine, it's really hard to decide what you're open to and what you're not. Especially knowing that the more selective you are, the longer it takes to get a baby. So if you're waiting for that perfect baby who's never been exposed to drugs, alcohol, cigarettes, or whatever else it might be, you're going to be waiting forever. There's no perfect case. It's adoption. It's messy.

Danny and I got through the list, for the most part, painlessly. We were on the same page for about 90 percent of the list. That remaining 10 percent, however, was tough.

Anyway, the point of having couples like us prespecify what we're open to is so that agency can begin to show our profile on our behalf, without our knowledge. That way if a birthmother comes into the agency and Reagan shows her Danny and my profile, and the birthmother is all "No way—they look like freaks," Danny and I will never know about it and be spared the heartache.

Like I said, though, adoption is messy and cases are rarely black and white enough for Reagan to know how to be able to act on our behalf. Most times she has to e-mail us to go over a detail or two about the case, ensuring we are indeed interested, which was precisely why she e-mailed us today. And guess what? We're interested. Maybe this will be the one?

Wednesday, October 5, 2011
ONE MONTH CHECKUP

While we waited to hear something about the case, I attended a follow up appointment at MD Anderson today. It started as they always do: getting my vitals taken by Dr. Alex's nurse, Allegra. Isn't that a pretty name? Admittedly a little less pretty ever since Allegra, the allergy drug, came on the market.

During the vitals assessing process, Allegra takes my height, weight, blood pressure, and temperature, all while I talk to her about Kim Kardashian and any other pop culture topics I see fit. Today we discussed the fishtail braid, which is currently my favorite thing to talk about, with Allegra or anyone else willing to engage in conversation about it. I love the fishtail braid and am terribly disappointed that I've yet to master the skill despite watching numerous YouTube tutorials. After we had reached a consensus that the fishtail braid is "the best thing ever," Allegra ushered me into a room where I was eventually greeted by Dr. Alex's nurse practitioner.

Though the nurse practitioner is not always the same person, this next part of the process is pretty typical and not entirely different than the game telephone. I basically have a proper appointment with the practitioner. She peeks at my incision and gives me a general once-over while inquiring about how it's going, health-wise. (I once made the mistake of not realizing she meant "health-wise" and told her how I was having a bad day because the Internet was down at my house.)

Upon answering the practitioner's questions, I get to ask a few of my own. The practitioner then leaves the room, tells Dr. Alex everything that was said, often right outside the door so I can hear the replay, and then Dr. Alex enters the room and says things like, "So I heard you have a question about hot flashes?"

See? Just like telephone. Or, depending on your experience, high school. I don't know why they do this. I suppose the practitioner is meant to be a buffer and save some of Dr. Alex's precious time. I'm sure there are annoying patients who go on and on about unnecessary nonsense, but I'm offended that they put me in that category. I get my commentary out of the way with Allegra. Give me some credit, people!

Today I wanted to ask Dr. Alex about the frequent hot flashes I've been having. Night sweats are definitely par for the course after surgery, at least for me. Dr. Bear once told me it was just the body's way of healing itself. The body works to recalibrate after a major surgery like mine, and hot flashes are just a byproduct of that. My night sweats, however, are now happening throughout my day. *All day*. Knowing that hot flashes are the most famous symptom of menopause, I was afraid this meant I was, indeed, in menopause.

Though my hot flashes are annoying, they're not the worst thing in the entire world. They're definitely something I can live with. Ever since I was diagnosed I feel like my biggest fears (aside from death) have been going bald from chemo or going into early menopause. I've had this idea in my head of what early menopause would be like. I picture my hair turning completely gray overnight, my face morphing into sixty-year-old me, and a hormone shift that would make me feel like a stranger in my own body.

While I'm not thrilled with the hot flashes or the fact that I'm likely in menopause, it's also liberating. It's like a weight has been lifted off of my shoulders. I'm facing my biggest fear and its okay. It's manageable. My life isn't over. There's nothing to fear but fear itself. I don't know who said that. Benjamin Franklin, maybe? But it's very apropos and true and, I'm sure, applicable to a much wider spectrum of fears than mine. So deep breath, everybody. You're stronger and braver than you give yourself credit for.

Dr. Alex said that she thinks it's too early to tell if I'm permanently in menopause. She said that she could prescribe a drug to help with the flashes, but said it was best to hold out on taking it so I could tell if the symptoms went away on their own. If I took the drug, I'd probably be a little less inconvenienced by the hot flashes, but I'd also have no insight into the progress my body was making. If any.

So that's what I decided to do. Wait it out. Hopefully three months from now I'll return to MD Anderson less sweaty, with a fishtail that even Lauren Conrad would envy.

2 COMMENTS

Marty:
Try FDR for that quote. Not Benjamin Franklin. As a history teacher, I'm offended. As your friend, I'm impressed you got as close as you did.

Megan replied:

Aww. Thanks Marty!

Monday, October 17, 2011

GIULIANA RANCIC

This morning I lay in bed and watched Giuliana Rancic, host of E! News, announce on the *Today Show* that she has cancer. I could tell by the expression on her face that her news wasn't going to be good, but I wasn't expecting cancer. I thought something more along the lines of infertility, as she's publicly struggled with that for years.

I yelled at the television as Giuliana said the word "cancer" to Ann Curry—nothing coherent really, just noise. Danny ran in from the bathroom where he was getting ready for work.

"What! What's wrong!" he demanded with a toothbrush in his mouth while Booker, the already nervous dog that he is, cowered on the bed next to me. I was upset. I was sad. I was mad.

Giuliana and her husband, Bill, have been pursuing rigorous fertility treatment for years. Prior to pursuing another round of IVF, however, one of her doctors insisted she get a mammogram—just as a precaution. To everyone's surprise, including my own, the image revealed she had breast cancer.

Despite eventually getting out of bed, turning off the television, showering, and working, I still feel like I still haven't fully moved on from Giuliana's news. It's like a big melancholy cloud has been hovering all day. I took Booker out for a walk late this afternoon and even then, seven hours later, a tear was rolling down my cheek.

I can't put my finger on what specifically about this is upsetting me so much. I mean, sure, I like Giuliana and all, but it's not like I know her personally. I've tried to be completely honest with myself and figure out what it is. Perhaps I'm just grieving for myself, vicariously, through her? With all the adoption stuff lately, the thought of someone thinking they're getting one step closer to having a baby, only to find out they're actually two steps further from it is heartbreaking to me. I've been there; I know how that feels.

I obviously want a biological child, to see how my personality and looks combined with Danny's translate into a child. It's a big loss. An enormous loss, actually. But for some reason I'm unable to grieve properly for it. Not that there's a "proper" way to grieve something like this. But you think I'd cry. Or yell. Or swear.* Or do something dramatic. But I haven't. For the most part I've just been positive about it, not focusing on what I can't control but on what I can.

Adoption isn't a cure for infertility. Sure it helps. It lessens the blow. But you still have to grieve the loss of your biological child—at least that's what we've been told at the prolific adoption orientations we've attended this past year. Perhaps Giuliana's news is serving as a catalyst to me in the grieving process.

At any rate, I'm sad today. Sad for Giuliana. Sad about her breast cancer. Sad she might never have the biological baby she wants so badly. And sad that I won't either.

On a lighter note (sorry for being Debbie Downer today), I will say that Giuliana's husband, Bill Rancic, is extremely, extremely sexy. At the very least, she has that going for her and that makes me feel better.

*Clarification: I do swear. But it has nothing to do with my infertility issues. Just lack of manners issues.

Wednesday, October 19, 2011
PIMPING OUT THE PAYROLL

I've hesitantly secured a temporary position with my family's company doing the payroll. Our payroll administrator, Nicole, is going on maternity leave, which is how this opportunity came about. I have a sneaking suspicion, however, this opportunity materialized based on my DNA as opposed to my skill set. I mostly think this because I'm awful at payroll.

Perhaps the reason I'm so terrible is that I found it challenging to concentrate during yesterday's training session via Skype. I wanted so badly to apply myself entirely. The truth is that when Nicole was attempting to teach me, I was completely preoccupied brainstorming alternative solutions to my actually having to do the payroll. Let me share what I came up with.

ALTERNATIVE SOLUTIONS TO MY DOING THE PAYROLL

- Outsource the payroll to India! I think a lot of companies do that now. Just send that shit right on over! (It's more convincing if you could see the sweeping arm gesture I'm doing when I say "send.")
- Two words: college intern.
- Prison work release program: preferably a white-collar, numbers-oriented criminal doing time for embezzlement but has since been reformed and "found God," ensuring he's not a repeat offender.
- Sell the company to "venture capitalists." (The first step? Learn what a "venture capitalist" is other than "what

Vince Vaughn and Owen Wilson pretended to be in *Wedding Crashers*," which is my current definition.)

- Not pay any of our employees during Nicole's absence and sell them on the ideology of "Mo' money, mo' problems."

1 COMMENT

Sean:

As a Kelsey Morgan employee, I'm not super comfortable with any of these "solutions."

Megan replied:

Mo' money, mo' problems, Sean!

Wednesday, October 26, 2011

BOOB JOB

I had an appointment today for an ultrasound of my boob. This was supposed to be a standard checkup to ensure the cyst in my boob isn't growing—and it's not! The ultrasound tech told me there were no changes in the cyst from last time. She said she needed to confirm with the radiologist to be sure, but assumed I could be on my way. All I had to do was return in six months for more imaging. Done and done.

So you can imagine my surprise when she came back five minutes later and reneged her statement. She said the radiologist "wanted it out" because of my medical history and young age. It was a slight blow. I mean, they aren't necessarily saying it's cancer, and a lumpectomy is only day surgery. But it's still surgery! My fourth surgery in seventeen months! And a surgery I wasn't anticipating!

After getting this news from radiology, Danny and I had two hours to kill before meeting with my breast doctor for supplemental information. Even though this news robbed us of any appetite, we grabbed lunch at the Rotary House, a sit-down restaurant located in MD Anderson. We laughed nervously over club sandwiches and a shared beer about what a shit show my health is.

When we did finally get the details from Dr. Blake, my breast doctor, it was pretty underwhelming. She had no new information. Just that there's no change in the mass, but based on my history, the radiologist who saw my imaging wants to be aggressive with the cyst.

Dr. Blake said that my case was controversial because I've had clean biopsies, which suggest the cyst is not worrisome. My age and history with ovarian cancer, however, suggest otherwise. Dr. Blake said that she wanted to present my case to her colleagues the following week. These meetings seem to be common practice for doctors—at least when I'm involved.

They're an opportunity for doctors to get their colleagues' opinions on cases that aren't black and white. Dr. Blake did say, however, that she'd be shocked if the board's recommendation was *not* a lumpectomy. She reminded me that the radiologist who read my imaging was the "head of the department" and implied that what this doctor says goes.

So that's where we're at. Dr. Blake will call me Tuesday after the meeting to confirm their recommendation of my lumpectomy. I'm not too worried about it, to be honest. The way I see it, there's no downside to doing the procedure. Worst-case scenario is that they find cancer, and even then the lumpectomy clearly will have been the right move. So feel free to regard this as "not that big of deal" because that's what I'm doing. Now if it's cancerous, it'll be a different story. A horror story, but we'll cross that bridge when we come to it.

I'll keep you all abreast (see what I did there) of my surgery date.

Tuesday, November 1, 2011
PROS AND CONS

Dr. Blake called today as promised. She actually called three times. I was too engaged in my Tracy Anderson workout DVD to hear her call the first two times. Good thing Dr. Blake is so persistent! (As is Tracy Anderson, which is less appreciated. Leg lifts for two minutes straight? I'd rather be fat, thanks.)

As it turns out, the tumor board at MD Anderson, arguably the most prestigious cancer hospital in the world, is stumped by my case. Stumped! I don't know whether to be proud or pissed. (I'm leaning towards proud.)

Dr. Blake explained to me that my case was even more controversial than she had anticipated going into the meeting. Initially, the board felt that I *wasn't* a candidate for a lumpectomy. Dr. Blake mentioned that the doctor who performed my biopsy earlier this year was actually at the meeting and felt extremely confident that they had cross-sectioned every single part of my cyst, finding zero cancer cells. I guess normally when doctors biopsy, they take about eight slides of tissue from a patient to sample. Know how many slides they took from me? Twenty! That is why this doctor is so confident. He told Dr. Blake, "If this cyst comes out, it's going to be benign." (I like him.) Based on this information, the board was comfortable recommending no lumpectomy as long as I repeated the imaging in six months.

Unfortunately Dr. Blake didn't stop there. She went on to say that, despite their certainty the cyst was benign, I should consider having the lumpectomy after all.

"Wait, what do you mean?!" I asked, surprised.

"Well," she said, "the other side of this is that you do have a slightly higher chance of developing breast cancer because of your medical history. Based on that, Dr. Lee, the radiologist who read your imaging, thinks a lumpectomy is best. We also considered how much this is going to make you crazy—having to get mammograms and ultrasounds every six months and worrying about it. Or if you were to ever be under another facility's care, it's likely they'd recommend you have it out immediately. So based on those things, it might be best to just have it done."

"Wait," I said, trying to understand what she was saying. "So what was the final decision by the board then? I'm confused. Are you telling me to do the lumpectomy or not?"

"Well," she said with a quick, nervous laugh, "we basically agreed that it could go either way. Everyone at the meeting was comfortable with you waiting another six months. But if you want to meet with a breast surgeon, you could do that too. Whatever you want to do."

"WHAT!" I exclaimed, now laughing nervously myself. "I don't know what to do. How am I supposed to know?"

Dr. Blake and I then talked in circles for another good ten minutes. By circles, I mean we kept talking about all the reasons I should have it done, followed by the reasons I shouldn't. Followed by the reasons I should. Followed by the reasons I shouldn't. Followed—okay, I'll stop, but that's truly what we did.

So that's where I'm at, friends. Never has the acronym WTF been more descriptive of my emotions. (Profound, I know.) My official decision for the time being is to not make a decision. I'm just going to go about life and hope that one day soon, when I least expect it, the answer will come to me. And because that probably won't happen, I did make an appointment with the breast surgeon—just to let him (her?) weigh in on this debate. Also, I figure a good way to decide could be to get information on the cosmetic effects of a lumpectomy. If it's really going to f-up my boob, then I'll be more apt to let it ride. But if the breast surgeon says the incision will be really minor, maybe I'll just do it (which is what Nike would tell me to do). Maybe it's a good thing nothing is happening on the adoption front right now—this nonsense is keeping us pretty busy.

Monday, November 21, 2011
BREAST SURGEON MEETING

Today I met with the breast surgeon. I began the appointment like any other one, by checking in with the front desk and getting my hospital bracelet placed around my wrist. This bracelet boasts my medical number, date of birth, and my picture—a heinous, terrible picture! You think being in a cancer hospital, surrounded by patients who are gravely ill, I'd check my shallowness at the door and not be bothered by frivolous things like a bad photo. Thinking that, of course, is wrong.

Now I'm going to get flack for this, so I'm prepared, but in my bracelet photo I look cognitively challenged. I know, I know—that's bad to say. At least give me points for being PC about it. I checked with my mom, a former Special Ed teacher, for the right term. (This is why I wanted to know, Mom!)

After agonizing over the picture for what seemed like hours, I decided to take matters into my own hands. I dramatically stood up, walked up to the front desk, and pleaded with the woman to retake my photo, all while Danny pretended he didn't know me.

Me: Excuse me, miss? I really hate this picture. Can we retake it?

Front Desk Lady: What do you want? A glamour shot?

Me: (Noting her sarcasm but choosing to ignore it) Yes, actually. Do you know how to do that? That'd be great!

Because of my new pic, my spirits were high as a nurse escorted me down the beige corridor of the breast unit. The picture wasn't a contender for my Facebook profile, but it was definitely one I could live with. My happiness was short lived, however, as I read the huge plaque I passed in the hallway. "This department was funded in memory of Lindsey Jones." The plaque went on to say that Lindsey was twenty-eight years old when she died of breast cancer. One year younger than me. My mood shifted after seeing that. This shit was a bigger deal than I was giving it credit for. I needed to take it more seriously.

My breast surgeon, Dr. Cats, (a woman) was a breath of fresh air when she walked into my room. She was high energy, friendly, and unlike her predecessors, not afraid to weigh in on what I should do.

Whenever presented with options in my medical care, I always ask my doctors "What would you do if you were me?" Answering this question, however, must be covered thoroughly in "Being a Doctor 101" because it's always sidestepped in a quick and professional manner. Never has a doctor given me a straight answer until today.

Without hesitation, Dr. Cats told me "If I were you, I'd probably resist the surgery for a little bit but then end up having it done. Because that's primarily what you're going to hear."

I wasn't sure if she meant "hear" from my doctors, or my family, or just, like, on the street. But either way I was pleasantly surprised by her candor and decided to have it done. Now I just have to decide on a date. Dr. Cats said she had an opening on December 13, and I got the feeling she didn't want that opening. She mentioned a few times that I could schedule for that particular date. It seems a little soon though—just a few weeks away. My body is still recovering from my last surgery with the hives and hot flashes and all. I told Dr. Cats I'd call her nurse tomorrow to get something on the books.

Tuesday, November 22, 2011
HAPPY ~~TURKEY~~ CHICKEN DAY!

Danny and I are in Austin for the holiday, spending it with his family. The drive to Austin from Houston is an interesting one as it's all country roads. This desolation makes for a candid country experience. For example, today I was afraid to enter the gas station we stopped at midtrip, as there was a chicken blocking the gas station's main entrance. A chicken! Just strutting, bobbing its head, making chicken noises—balk, balk, balk!

The other patrons were laughing at me, finding my angst amusing, as they breezed by the chicken and entered or exited with their snacks in tow. But not me. I'm from Chicago. In

Chicago, we don't get that close to chickens unless we're eating them. Every time I tried to make a run for the door, the chicken would come towards me, the little bastard.

Something similar happened a few months ago when I dropped Booker off at the kennel in Pearland, Texas. Pearland is a few miles out of Houston. It's a relatively large, thriving suburb. Yet that didn't stop me from seeing a dead HORSE on the side of the road! Not a deer, or a skunk, or something routine. A fucking horse! It's not normal! Nor is a chicken at gas station. Come on, Texas, let's class it up a bit, shall we?

Thankfully Danny came and interrupted me from playing chicken with the chicken (too easy?) by handing me my cell phone. "It's MD Anderson," he said as he gave it to me.

"Hello," I said tentatively.

"Hi, Megan. This is Noel. I work with Dr. Cats. I got your message about scheduling your surgery sometime in February. We are relatively open that month, so it's up to you. We operate on Tuesdays and Thursdays. I could do February 14 or 16 if you like."

"Uh, let's go with the sixteenth," I said, not wanting to have surgery on Valentine's Day.

"The sixteenth it is. Very good, Megan. You'll probably need to come in on the fifteenth for your pre-op appointment, but we'll contact you about that as the date approaches. Sound good?"

"Yep. Sounds good. Thank you," I answered and hung up the phone.

Simple as that. My lumpectomy is scheduled. I got back in the car and decided I could wait to pee until I got to Austin. Stupid ass chicken.

Tuesday, December 6, 2011
GIULIANA RANCIC, PART 2

This morning I woke up to a missed call from my Mom. I also had two e-mails from my cousin Brenna, neither of which had text in them, just links to *People* magazine's website. Clearly something had happened in the celeb world—I just didn't know what. I thought perhaps something with Kim Kardashian, because let's be honest, it's always Kim. The minute I clicked on the first link, however, my heart sank. *Giuliana Rancic Announces Double Mastectomy on the Today Show*. Ugh.

Instead of reading the article I tried to find the video online. It was easy. I watched as Giuliana and her husband, Bill, sat there and gave the details. Her double lumpectomies weren't able to produce clean margins. This meant she could do either radiation or the double mastectomy. There were obvious pros and cons to both scenarios, but she's opted for a double mastectomy. Well played, Giuliana. I would too.

I had several thoughts and emotions as I took in the news, the first, of course, being sadness. As I mentioned, I seem to have taken an emotional interest in Giuliana. After giving it more thought, I think it's because she's the first person I've felt connected to, or an affinity for, since being diagnosed with cancer. She's likeable, relatable, fun, and relatively young. Cancer needs more spokespeople like her.

The last time I was at MDA, there was a massive display of quilts. Each quilt was hung up next to another, lining the pedestrian walkway that connects two hospital wings together. No exaggeration—there must have been hundreds of quilts! According to a small sign near the display, the quilts were all made in honor of spreading awareness for ovarian cancer. While quilts are nice (I guess?), I had a hard time feeling any sort of connection to the display despite ovarian cancer being my own disease. I mean, they're quilts.

The one positive thing about hearing Giuliana's news, however, is that I feel slightly reassured I'm making the right decision regarding my own lumpectomy. The doctors guiding me have been so ambiguous about it. I hate the fact that I'll be going into the procedure not 100 percent sure that it's necessary. But clearly, this shit isn't anything to play around with, and Giuliana is a testament to that.

4 COMMENTS

Janet:
Small quilts are often sent to cancer wards for warmth and comfort for the chemo patients.

Megan replied:
I didn't know that. I feel bad now.

Danny:
You should.

Megan replied:
Shut up, Danny!

Wednesday, January 4, 2012
HAPPY NEW YEAR

I thought the timing of today's appointment with Dr. Alex was perfect. Everyone wants to start off the new year healthy and fit.

Take Danny for example. He's on a big New Year's diet. He's reading special diet books and everything. Yesterday he asked me if I knew that "you're supposed to eat more than one fruit and vegetable a day." "Uhh. *Yeah*," I said. "You didn't?"

Today's appointment started with an ultrasound of my stomach/ovarian area. A little Asian woman, who's actually done ultrasounds of me before, greeted me as she walked in the super dark, cold room. "You!" she said, handing me a warm blanket and inadvertently reminding me English was her second language.

I lay on the table, fairly relaxed given what was happening, as she tapped away on her ultrasound keyboard. I wanted to read a magazine or my Twitter feed on my phone as she did her thing, but I thought that might be weird. Instead I tried to focus on her facial expressions, typing movements, and even the screen itself to see if I could piece together the verdict of what she was seeing. Of course I learned nothing other than that the resemblance between my insides and outer space is uncanny.

Upon finishing my ultrasound, the lady told me she was going to speak with the radiologist and see if we needed supplemental pictures. Assuming we would, I was surprised when she returned five minutes later and told me to get dressed.

"Really?" I asked cautiously, surprised.

"Yes."

"So, how'd I do? Did you see anything?" I asked.

"Two cysts ovary. But you bleed. Could be that."

Ugh, I thought. Not good. I got dressed and went downstairs to the diagnostic lab to do my CA-125. Another prerequisite to seeing Dr. Alex. It's funny how much I've learned after being in the cancer game for a while. For so long I just did what my hospital schedule print-out told me, having no idea why. Now I know that this CA-125 test, in addition to the ultrasound, are the tools Dr. Alex needs in order to advise me. Without them,

Dr. Alex's guess is as good as mine. (Well, it's probably a little bit better than mine.)

The diagnostic lab is a trip. It's like its own private world right smack in the middle of MD Anderson. The lab has its own waiting room, and when your name is called you're escorted back into what feels like the movie set of *The Help*. It's a bustling area of black, middle-aged, female phlebotomists. They all call me "Sugar" as they stick me with a needle, take vials of blood, and patch me up with a Band-Aid. They might even ask where I'm from, but usually they talk amongst themselves, always issuing a deep, hearty *mmm-hmm* when something resonates with them. It's fantastic.

With an hour to go to my scheduled appointment time, I went up to the sixth floor to wait to see Dr. Alex. Again, now being the experienced cancer patient that I am, I had my laptop with me so I could get some things done during what would surely be a super long wait. Eventually my girl, Allegra, called my name and invited me back to take my vitals. We of course discussed Kim Kardashian and her seventy-two-day marriage. (Allegra thinks it was all for publicity. I'm not so sure.)

Next Dr. Alex's practitioner and nurse came in my room to get me ready for Dr. Alex. For as time efficient as MD Anderson attempts to be, it's surprising that waiting is such a common occurrence. For example, today when Dr. Alex entered the room, her nurse already had me on the table, legs in the stirrups, and butt scooched to the end of the table. It wasn't until this was all completed that she knocked on the door from the inside, signaling for Dr. Alex to enter.

After a quick, though horribly invasive, examination, Dr. Alex told me I could sit up so we could chat.

"I think you're good!" she said, enthusiastically. "It's great that you no longer have the hot flashes. And your ultrasound looked good." (Earlier, I had told the practitioner that my hot flashes had subsided.)

"Really?" I said, surprised. "I thought they saw two cysts during the ultrasound."

"Yeah, but the makeup of those cysts isn't worrisome. They're really simple."

"Huh," I said tentatively. "Great."

"I haven't received your CA-125 results yet, but I'll call you when I do. Other than that, we'll have you come back in three months for more imaging."

"Cool," I said.

"Any other questions or anything?" she asked.

"Well. I did just want to discuss my lumpectomy with you," I said.

"Yeah, I saw that in your notes," she answered, tilting her head for me to go on.

"Basically, there was some controversy about whether or not I needed the procedure. I guess I just want to know what you think. I mean, I'm fine having the surgery if I need it. But I also don't want to do it just to do it. You know?" I asked, hoping she did indeed "know."

"Yeah. I was reading some of your doctor's notes. The thing is—one in eight women in this country has breast cancer. So the lumpectomy could be a good thing for you to do because at least you'll know . . . blah, blah, blah, blah."

She wasn't saying blah. She was saying tons of pertinent stuff but I was distracted by my grumbling stomach. *I'm hungry. Pizza sounds good. I'm gonna get pizza from the cafeteria when this is over. I can't believe Dr. Alex is so pretty with no makeup. I wish I looked that good without makeup.*

"Megan. Are you listening? Do you have any other questions?" she asked.

"Oh. Uh, no. Cute hair." I said, smiling convincingly, admiring the back of her new shoulder-length bob as she left the room.

Thursday, January 5, 2012
SCOUTED

Dr. Alex called me twice last night with the results of my CA-125. But being the idiot I am, I screened her call both times. An intelligent person would have thought, *Huh, 312-789-6666—I don't know that number, but I'll answer it anyway. Especially the second time because I'm expecting important test results from my doctor.*

I, on the other hand, thought, *312-789-6666—hmm, that looks vaguely familiar, but I can't be interrupted right now. I'm too busy watching* Scouted *on E!—an amazing show about high school girls becoming runway models! Maybe I'll be scouted one day!*

Doctor Alex called a third time while Danny and I were en route to Whole Foods to pick up something for dinner. I answered the phone nervously and listened as she told me my CA-125 blood results were "elevated." Elevated is bad.

Dr. Alex gave me options, which I always appreciate. She said I could come in right away for a CT scan to get better pictures of the ovary. Or I could wait six weeks and repeat the test, in hopes that the elevated results are due to my menstrual cycle, just like the ultrasound tech had mentioned when she said, "You bleed."

"I mean, if you are okay with me waiting six weeks, I will," I said tentatively.

"I am," she said in a way that made she think she was writing something down. "Nothing is going to change much within six weeks. I'm comfortable waiting, but call me back if you're worried or anything."

"Okay," I said, now starting to really worry, especially since she said that.

Maybe screening her call was the right move after all?

3 COMMENTS

Kimmy Lynn:
I love *Scouted* too. Such a quality program!

Megan replied:
This might be morbid, but I've decided that if my cancer ever became terminal, and I was accepted into the Make-A-Wish program, which I'm pretty sure is just for kids, but whatever, my wish would be to go on *Scouted*. Wouldn't that be so amazing?

Kimmy Lynn:
I mean, the *Scouted* part would. The fact that you were dying wouldn't be great.

Megan replied:
True.

Thursday, January 19th, 2012
ADOPTION UPDATE

Last week I got a call from our Reagan, who told me she'd shown our profile to a birthmother and she wanted to meet us!

Before I go any further, maybe I should give a brief, crash course on adoption. I mean, adoption once you get to this point in the process. A crash course on adoption, as a whole, would read longer than *War and Peace*. (Know what's weird? I have no working knowledge of *War and Peace* other than the fact that it's a long-ass book. Who wrote it? No idea. What's it about? Well, probably war . . . then peace. But other than that, I know nothing! Yet it's still an innate reference that I use. Strange, right?)

Anyway, Danny and I are pursuing an "open" adoption. An open adoption means we will have some sort of relationship with the birthmother of our future child. We have no idea what this relationship will look like. Perhaps we'll meet for dinner once a year? Maybe we'll never meet in person but exchange pictures via e-mail. It's possible we'll never meet. It's equally possible that we'll be Facebook friends. Danny and I have no idea. All we know is we're open to whatever and will just see how everything plays out.

The birthmother picks the adoptive family though—not the other way around. For some reason, people are weirded out when we tell them that. I'm not sure why. That's pretty standard as far as adoption goes. Danny and I had to put together a "profile" about our life together: pictures of us, pictures of Booker, pictures of our home—all with captions and brief paragraphs giving insight into what our life is like.

That way, when a birthmother is considering adoption, the agency can provide her with four or five profiles of potential families for her baby. If she does decide on adoption, she can choose two, maybe three, of those families from the profiles to actually meet. Upon doing that, she'll eventually decide on a couple to be the adoptive parents. At that point you're considered "matched" and you can begin communicating with your birthmother, independent of the agency. That's a really simplified, perfect scenario. There are usually more twists and turns involved—including the fact that 25 percent of the time the birthmother changes her mind after being matched. So that's terrifying. But that's an overview of the general process.

Back to that phone call I received last week from Reagan. About (cough for emphasis) twins! Reagan told me very nonchalantly that they were working with a nineteen-year-old birthmother (and her eighteen-year-old boyfriend, the birthfather) who were pregnant with twin boys. This couple, because of their age, knew they weren't financially or emotionally ready to parent a baby, let alone two. They had seen our profile and wanted to meet us, in addition to two other couples this coming weekend. Reagan asked if we were available for dinner Sunday night, as they were meeting the other couples Friday and Saturday.

"Yeah, that will work," I told Reagan calmly, despite the fact that my head was spinning, primarily with excitement. *We have to drive to Austin. Who are the other two couples we're competing against? I need to cancel our dinner plans for Saturday. Twins? Holy fucking shit! I should call Danny.* How I was going to survive seventy-two more hours of this mind racing, I had no idea.

When Sunday night eventually rolled around, Danny and I found ourselves at a restaurant that we would never have been at had we not been meeting the birthparents of our potential children. There was nothing wrong with the restaurant, it was just in the middle of nowhere and felt sort of TGI Friday's–esque, even though the food appeared to be Mexican. Maybe it was just all the flair that our waiter was sporting.

Danny and I arrived at the restaurant early and pretended to watch the NFL playoffs that were playing in the restaurant's bar as we waited for the birthparents. At least I did—Danny probably really was watching the game. I stared at the door, on the lookout for pregnant teenagers. There was no mistaking them as they walked in the door. The girl was hugely preggo and her boyfriend looked just like he did in the picture Reagan had e-mailed me earlier so we'd know who to look for in this exact moment.

The dinner was awkward, even more so than I expected it to be. These kids were kids, first of all. You hear eighteen and nineteen and think, well, that's technically adults. But these were kids. They talked about what their parents would and wouldn't let them do and about the fights they had with their siblings over video games.

The age difference made it tough for us to find common ground, but their personalities made it challenging as well. These two weren't your classic high school couple. They didn't have the football player and cheerleader captain vibe going on, nor were they the homecoming king and queen. (Fun fact! Danny and I were homecoming royalty at our own respective high schools! Ha! Glory days!) Instead, Eliza and Scotty appeared to be the introverted, art students that I'm sure every high school has some version of. My hopes of talking about high school sports, extracurriculars, *American Idol*, and any other lighthearted subjects I envisioned gossiping over appeared to be out the window.

Danny and I tried our damndest to come up with conversation starters: Twilight, the Hunger Games, food, even cooking. But these only generated two or three uninterrupted minutes of conversation tops.

It was tough. Especially during the two times that there was dead air for at least a minute. Keep in mind that Danny, salesman extraordinaire, was unofficially leading this dinner. He takes nerdy paralegals and pretentious attorneys out to lunch all the time, so he's awesome in these types of forced scenarios. Plus, I like to think that I'm a pretty social person myself. So if we were struggling, how did the other couples fare? How does *anyone* fare in this situation? I'm not blaming these kids. They appeared to be good kids, obviously. They were choosing adoption—a selfless act, especially when millions of kids in their situation choose to abort. The fact that Eliza and Scotty were sitting with us, at dinner, reflected immensely on their character. But the whole thing was still awkward for both parties.

On the way home from dinner I was exhausted. For three days I'd had been anticipating this dinner, wondering what was it going to be like. Were they going to pick us? Was I going to be a momma to twins? Now that it was over I was physically and emotionally drained. I tilted my seat back in Danny's Tahoe and just lay there. I had no idea if they were going to pick us. I told Danny I wouldn't be surprised if they did, nor would I be surprised if they didn't. But it was over; there was nothing we could do now but wait and see.

They didn't pick us. We were apparently their second choice of the three couples they met with. We didn't find that out for another four days (that's ninety-six hours). I was sad. I cried. I don't know why I was sad. I wholeheartedly believe that Danny and I will end up with the baby we are meant to end up with. I genuinely believe that with every fiber of my being. Those two teenagers weren't the birthparents of my baby. But I was still sad. So was Danny. I also felt bad for our family and friends who knew what was going on. I had told my cousin, Jess. My brother. My parents. Danny's mom knew and was so excited. Not only was I disappointed for myself, but I knew they were going to be disappointed too.

I'm not sharing this with all of you to make you sad. So don't be sad, people. Danny and I aren't even sad anymore. I'm sharing it, I suppose, because this is all part of my story. I've come this far in sharing and documenting my ups and downs with the world. I'm not helping anyone, including myself, by omitting the tougher parts. It just so happened that this past week was one of those "tougher parts."

I also am motivated to share this particular experience in hopes that somewhere out there, one of you is encouraged by it. Not encouraged to adopt—this is hardly a commercial for the process—but perhaps encouraged in your own adoption experience.

Hearing firsthand from others going through similar experiences, whether it be cancer or adoption, is always encouraging for me. Nothing beats meeting a fellow patient at the hospital and having a really meaningful conversation and connection. We don't even have to swap sob stories; just knowing that we're both coming from the same place is enough. Same goes for adoption. I love talking to other couples in the process. I much prefer that than talking to someone who's already successfully adopted. That, at this point, when you're still in the thick of it, is almost annoying. I'm still in the thick of it, people—shout out to anyone else who is too.

Wednesday, February 15, 2012
PRE-OP PARTY!

Today was the pre-op for my lumpectomy, and it went really well. Not only did I make my necessary rounds in less than four hours (lab work, anesthesiologist, nurse, surgeon), but I also have a much better sense of what's going to happen tomorrow. First and foremost, I learned that I'm not having a lumpectomy. Ha! I lied to you all about that. My bad.

What I'm actually having is an excisional biopsy. It's basically the same thing. My nurse even told me that some (lesser) hospitals will use the term interchangeably. (She didn't say lesser. I did.) A lumpectomy refers to the removal of a known cancerous cyst. Because my cyst is *not* cancerous (knock on wood) the procedure is called an excisional biopsy. This same nurse went on to tell me more about what to expect.

"So, Megan, tomorrow, before anything else, you'll come here and we'll do some imaging to 'pin' the spot. That way when the surgeon goes in she won't have to look for the spot, she'll know exactly where it's at."

"Okay."

"So we'll put a needle in the cyst and then cover it with a Styrofoam cup to protect it. Then we'll take you down to anesthesiology."

"That cup part sounds ghetto but okay."

"Ha! I suppose. But we've been doing it that way for years. Sometimes old is gold. From there it's pretty easy. Once you're done in anesthesia, Dr. Cats will surgically remove the cyst. She is really good. She's known for her very small stitches, so you'll be in good hands."

"Okay."

"Any other questions, Megan?"

"What can I expect in terms of pain?"

"Well, you'll go home with a prescription for Norco or Vicodin or something like that, but every patient is different. For some patients Tylenol is sufficient."

"Yeah, I'll take the Norco." I said, unable to fathom who wouldn't. It's the one perk in all of this. (Not to be confused with Percocet, which would be cool too.)

"Do we find out tomorrow if it's cancer?" I asked, assuming we would.

"No. We have to run the pathology in the lab, so we'll know within seven to ten days."

"What?!" I said, surprised and louder than I intended. "That seems long like a long time!"

"Well, it might be sooner, but we'll let you know as soon as we know," she assured me.

I'm still confused about why we won't find out about the cancer tomorrow. In my past surgeries, the pathology came back immediately so my doctors knew which way to proceed in the respective surgery. But for this it'll be ten days? Again, something I should have asked the nurse, but I was too preoccupied thinking about the whole Styrofoam nonsense. It's bizarre, right? Not to mention very environmentally unsound. Al Gore clearly hasn't caught wind of this.

Overall though, the procedure sounds pretty easy breezy. Especially since I don't have to do that God-awful prep tonight. I can eat up until midnight, which is fantastic, especially since my friend, Jess, just dropped off some Rice Krispie treats. Danny's mom is also coming into town for the surgery and rumor has it she's bringing her chocolate chip cookies.

Saturday, February 18, 2012
BOOB JOB SUCCESS

I continue to be pleasantly surprised by how easy this whole thing has been. I think I've been comparing it too much to my previous surgery, which is silly. It's apples and oranges; I know that now.

My day started nice and early yesterday as Danny, his mom, and I were at the hospital by 7:00 a.m. sharp. We rode the elevator up to the fourth floor and shared it with a girl who seemed my age, from what I could tell, at least. She was fully covered, with the exception of her eyes, in an abaya. (An abaya is the robe thing some Islamic women wear. Think *Sex in the City 2*!)

I was completely fascinated by this girl. I looked down at my own outfit, noting the drastic difference in our clothing, mine consisting of black Target yoga pants and a purple Victoria's Secret hoodie. I've actually seen a lot of female patients at MD Anderson wearing abayas but have never stood just inches away from one, able to hear her every breath. I wondered if this girl minded wearing her abaya. I wondered if she was about to have the same surgery as me. I wondered if she was as interested in my outfit as I was hers. I silently wished her well.

I checked in for surgery by giving my name to a woman sitting behind the "Surgery Check-In" counter and printing my name on her roll call list. She then sent me over to the same part of the hospital that I routinely go to for mammograms and ultrasounds. So far, it felt like I was there for another routine doctor's appointment, not surgery. Quickly enough, I was called back by a nurse, Kelly, who'd performed a few of my mammograms previously. We both gave each other a look of recognition.

"Hey!" I said.

"Hey!" she said. "I remember you."

Kelly and a friendly little radiologist man quickly got to work on me. I was put in the mammogram machine. After taking a series of pictures, they inserted a long but incredibly thin needle into my boob. It didn't hurt at all because they'd already shot me up with some numbing medicine. The whole thing was pretty simple and quick. So simple that the three of us chatted throughout the process as though we were having coffee and not preparing for the OR.

The radiologist man then left the room after wishing me good luck. As soon as he shut the door behind him, Kelly got to work on the highly anticipated procedure of taping the cup onto my boob.

"My pre-op nurse yesterday told me you were going to do this," I said to Kelly as she took a few strips of athletic tape and carefully placed them over the cup until it was secure. "And I told her that it sounded extremely ghetto."

"I know, right?" she laughed. "I've been doing mammograms for twenty years, and this is the one thing about the process that hasn't changed. We used something else for a while from some medical supplier, but it just didn't work as well as the cup."

Kelly then made me sit in a wheelchair and pushed me back to a little makeshift room, where three of the four walls were actually curtains. She hugged me good-bye, careful not to bump the cup.

"Good luck, sweetie. I prayed for you. I pray for all my patients, so I know you'll be okay."

After sitting idly for a whole six seconds, I started texting Danny pictures of myself, partly to keep myself busy and partly because I'm vain and send him pictures of myself frequently. Soon another nurse popped her head in from behind the curtain and asked who was accompanying me today. She was going to retrieve them so we all could go down to the OR together.

Before I knew it, I was being wheeled down an empty hallway by a nurse with Danny and his mom trailing closely behind. It was pretty interesting, actually, as we were traveling through the "employees only" part of the hospital. I saw nurses eating their lunches and idle elliptical and stretching machines, I assumed for doctors to use between surgeries.

Upon getting to the next room, Danny's mom had to leave as I was allowed just one other person to wait with me. My nurse left too, upon instructing me to get in the bed and put on the compression stockings and hair net that were laid out on the bed. She said someone would be in shortly to give further instruction. I'm not sure to whom specifically she was referring because there were tons of people who came in to greet me: my anesthesiologist, my anesthesiologist's assistant, my surgeon, my surgeon's assistant, Kevin Bacon. (Ha! Because Kevin Bacon is in everything!)

Of all the people bustling in and out of my room, asking me things, injecting me with things, wrapping me with things, my surgeon's assistant was the most memorable. She couldn't have been much older than me and was a cute girl.

"Okay, Megan, let's talk about post-surgery. You are going to wake up in a surgi-bra. You are going to need to wear this for the first forty-eight hours upon waking up. I need my surgery site to be compressed for at least that long," she said firmly.

"Okay."

"No showers for forty-eight hours either. I need my surgery site to stay dry."

"Cool."

"No baths for two weeks. I don't know if you're a bath person, but I don't want my surgery site soaking in stuff."

"Right."

"Any other questions?" she asked.

"Nope."

She then excused herself from the room in order to go find and check in with Dr. Cats. I looked over at Danny.

He gave me a weak smile and looked nervous. I didn't have time to tell him to "relax" or "don't be nervous," though, because one of my nurses, wearing New Orleans–themed scrubs, told him to kiss me good-bye.

Though I don't recall them doing so, they must have injected my anesthesia at some point because I suddenly felt fantastic— warm, happy, and relaxed. You only have a minute or two at the most to enjoy the anesthesia before you're knocked out completely. I remember once making it into the OR and still being conscious.

I started to freak out that the anesthesia hadn't worked and that they were going to start anyway. I started screaming, "I'M AWAKE! I'M AWAKE!" and everyone just looked at me like, *Uh, yeah. We know.* Thank God I passed out seconds later, so the embarrassment was short-lived.

Yesterday, however, I had no memories of the OR. I just remember being pushed back, slowly but surely, into oblivion.

Saturday, February 25, 2012

BEACH BOOBS

I'm so pleasantly surprised with the scar that my lumpectomy/ excisional biopsy (whatever you want to call it) has left. It's not bad at all. I was expecting a big chunk to be missing from my boob and for it, overall, to be not cute. But it's really not bad. The shape of my boob is completely the same—now it just has a super thin, one-inch scar framing the top of it. I even tried on my J. Crew bikini this morning and the scar was 100 percent concealed. Danny walked in the bedroom while I was in the midst of changing.

"What are you doing?" he asked.

"What does it look like I'm doing? Going to the beach!" I answered him, facetiously, which I thought was obvious.

"Really?" he asked, genuinely surprised.

"No!" I said, laughing. "It's like 9:00 a.m. and super cold out and I don't even know where a beach is."

He then left the room without saying anything, probably because he felt dumb. Or thought I was a bitch. Most likely both.

I took one last look in the mirror before changing back into my clothes that Booker had now sprawled out on. I was fine with the way my boob(s) looked in the bikini—there was virtually no difference than before my surgery. It was my stomach that was holding me back from a true Rachel Bilson beach bod. And I'm not even talking about the scars. My scars don't bother me nearly as much as my abs—or should I say a lack thereof. I wrestled Booker for my shirt and thought about how I should channel this whole experience into workout inspiration.

"That's it," I told Booker. "We're going on diet. No carbs, no sugar, no bones—the whole kitten caboodle."

Though I suppose in the grand scheme of things, my "thick" stomach is a champagne problem (no champagne either) because I found out yesterday, drumroll please, that not only did my lumpectomy come back "clean" but that my CA-125 that I've since retaken is good to go too. I'm officially, at least for the time being, cancer free in both places.

4 COMMENTS

Mom:
Congrats, honey, but the expression is *kit and caboodle*. Not "kitten caboodle."

Danny:
Ha! Whose dumb now?

Megan replied:
You are, Danny. It's *who's*, not *whose*!

Danny replied:
Dammit!

part three

Saturday, September 15, 2012
SARAH

I think Danny and I met the birthmother of our child. And, if that's not CRAZY enough for y'all, you should know she's due next week.

If you're all "*Wait, what?*" then you know how we feel. We have no idea what is going on—I mean technically we do, I guess, it's just hard to believe. About two weeks ago we received news that two birthmothers that had seen our profile within the same week. I was excited by this activity as I assumed it was a sign we were moving up on the list, but never did I think we'd actually get picked. I guess I forgot that's a possibility in this whole adoption game.

Friday night we had a very brief phone call with Sarah, a prospective birthmother who apparently wanted to speak with us only and nobody else. (A great sign obviously!) The call was pretty brief, partly because the purpose of the call was primarily to set up an in-person meeting. It was also brief because the connection was terrible. Had an operator been eavesdropping on our call, they would never guessed that Danny and I were talking to the woman who is (hopefully) the future mother of our child, but rather thought we were reenacting that annoying Sprint commercial.

Sarah: Can you hear me now?
Me: Uh.
Sarah: Wait . . . Can you hear me now?
Me: Sorta.
Sarah: How 'bout now? Can you hear me now?

We were eventually able to confirm that we'd meet at the adoption agency on Monday afternoon. I also managed to ask

Sarah if she knew what the sex of the baby was, assuming she didn't. I figured if she did know it would have been on the extensive paperwork we received.

"Yeah!" she said, surprised by my cluelessness. "It's a girl! You guys didn't know? I thought y'all knew!"

"A girl?" I said, repeating it aloud to myself more than anyone else. "Oh my gosh!" Truthfully, I had always told people that I'd prefer a boy. Partly because I'm afraid of teenage girls. For real. They scare me. Have you guys seen *Gossip Girl*? Those high school bitches don't play. But whatever. It's a baby girl! It's amazing! Besides, who knows how real this is yet. It's way too soon to be getting our hopes up. I mean, yes, it looks really good, but we still have a ways to go. Twenty-five percent of the time they change their mind.

Monday, September 17, 2012
SHOP 'TIL WE DROP

We arrived at the adoption agency a little before 2:00 p.m., the time we'd arranged to meet Sarah. The agency is actually just a tiny little house converted into office space in the Southside area of Austin. Danny and I were nervously chatting up Reagan and grilling her with last-minute questions when we heard Sarah knock at the front door. Reagan went to go get Sarah as Danny and I remained in the room and tried not to have heart attacks.

I heard Reagan open the door to find a crying Sarah. Reagan quickly ushered her into her office and I got a glimpse of Sarah's back, flip-flops, and the burnt orange dress she was wearing. I guess it didn't matter what she looked like, though—the crying made me assume it was a no-go. She had already changed her mind—why else would she be crying? I looked at Danny and could tell he thought so too. "Let's just go," I said, half pissed that we'd driven all this way just to be jerked around, half relieved that we didn't have to go through what was sure to be an incredibly intense meeting.

Before I could convince Danny to go, however, Reagan came in and told us that Sarah just needed a minute. She was nervous and emotional, but she was in fact coming in to meet us.

Sarah walked in, and my first thought was, *YES! She looks normal!* Maybe that sounds weird, but for me—and likely for all adoptive parents honest enough to admit it—worrying about what your child will look like is par for the course. And it's always the worst case scenario that you imagine. I never see a super cute kid and think, *Huh, I wonder if that's how my baby will look.* It's always, like, the ugliest baby you've ever seen in your life, or the super fat, annoying, bad-mannered kid at the post office who makes your stomach sink and you think, *Shit, that's totally gonna be my kid. Everyone is going to hate them—I know I do.* Rationally, you know it doesn't matter and that you'll love your kid no matter what, but irrationally, you're afraid you'll end up with Honey Boo Boo. (Though I realize some people would like that. In which case feel free to come up with your own analogy.)

Reagan initiated the conversation between Sarah, Danny, and me. She asked Sarah what she had liked about our profile and why she picked us. Sarah said one of the main reasons she had picked us was because we were Christian—that was really important to her and the birthfather (who was not able to attend the meeting but was supportive of the adoption).

I was surprised by this. I didn't remember our profile saying we were Christian. I mean, I suppose that's how I'd explain ourselves, Danny especially, who is more strong in his faith than I. But I specifically remember purposely not mentioning anything about religion on our profile. So many of the sample profiles the agency had showed us at orientation were rampant with references to Jesus and "adoption being their calling" and blah, blah, blah. That wasn't really my style. I did make a mental note, however, to work it into the conversation that Danny's brother is a minister in Virginia. Just saying.

Danny then took the floor per Reagan's soft moderation of the conversation. He told Sarah very general stuff about us. That we're from Chicago, we live in Houston, all fluff basically that Sarah should have already knew about us from our profile. And we knew all the vital stuff about her from hers. I suppose this exercise though was more a matter of us being in the same room with one another, getting comfortable with each other, and everyone practicing managing their nerves than it was about exchanging pertinent information.

What was I nervous about? Everything. Nervous Sarah had no intention of going through with this adoption and that Danny and I were in for a world of hurt. Nervous that Sarah did plan on going through with the adoption yet at the last second would change her mind, unbeknownst to her now. Nervous that the birthfather wouldn't sign his papers even though he'd already verbally agreed to it.

I will say, however, that the longer we were in that room, the more comfortable we all got, so much so that Reagan eventually excused herself and let the three of us fend for ourselves. Sarah asked me if I had a nursery ready for the baby. I told her that I didn't. I was afraid she'd take that as a sign that I didn't really want a baby, so I immediately told her the reason why: That it would be too painful, too depressing, too awful to have a constant reminder in our house of the baby we didn't have. She seemed genuinely empathic. She went on to ask the obvious follow-up question, which was why Danny and I couldn't have children on our own. I held my breath as I said the word cancer. I was afraid Sarah would have the same concern that the BSA agency had, that I wasn't healthy enough to parent a baby if I'd had cancer. But Sarah didn't even raise an eyebrow; on the contrary, she continued to be empathetic. It was a huge burden that I could let go of, and I could feel myself begin to really take a liking to Sarah.

Eventually we were the ones bombarding Sarah with questions. We asked her about her other children. (Sarah doesn't have the means to provide for them, let alone this baby, which is why she's making this adoption plan.) We asked more about the baby's birthfather—how they met, what he's like, his thoughts about the adoption, and his family. Sarah had me feel her belly, and I felt the baby kick. Part of me was thrilled with excitement and part of me was terrified because I had now felt the baby kick. I didn't want to know what it felt like to not get the baby that you'd felt kick. It was getting harder and harder to maintain my emotional walls, and that scared me.

The three of us talked and talked and talked—we were in that room for over two hours. Danny even managed to work football into the conversation. Having lived in Texas all her life, Sarah likes both Texas teams, the Texans and the Cowboys. Danny joked that that was a deal breaker, that Sarah needed to be a Chicago Bears fan. We all laughed as the tension in the room continued to deteriorate. (Though my laugh was half-hearted as I'd seen Danny setting up the joke from a mile away.)

We were in that room for so long that it eventually began to feel normal—normal to be sitting in a room with this virtual stranger talking about how we'd raise her baby. It also felt right. We had a good rapport with Sarah. Though she was only twenty-seven, she was an old soul. She was easy to talk to and her love for the baby was undeniable, obviously. We wouldn't have been in this room with her if she didn't love this baby. Sarah, or any birthmother who chooses an adoption plan for their baby, could have easily chosen to get an abortion. And not only did Sarah love this baby, but she loved the baby's father. They've been together for six years, a sign of their love and commitment. Sarah wanted what was best for her baby even though that meant not getting to raise her herself. Just like Sarah had developed empathy for me, I had developed empathy for her. We shared a box of Kleenex throughout the session accordingly.

Toward the end of our meeting, Sarah mentioned several times that she'd not been able to go to the grocery store lately, having no car and being too pregnant to ride the bus with arms full of groceries. Despite the rumblings in my stomach (this time due to hunger as opposed to nerves) we offered to take Sarah to the store on our way home. The three of said good bye to Reagan, (who was completely unphased by our collective departure), and Danny helped a very pregnant Sarah get into the backseat of his Tahoe. From the backseat she began to navigate our way to the store. I asked her what music she wanted to listen to for the ride, and she told me Garth Brooks, which was fine by me—Garth Brooks is the man.

Danny stayed in the car to participate in a conference call while Sarah and I did her grocery shopping in a Walmart. I'm not a Walmart aficionado or anything, but I've been in a handful before and this one was by far the nicest I'd ever been in. I grabbed the cart, and Sarah and I began to chitchat like old college friends as we navigated the frozen food section. I realized that grocery shopping is a fairly intimate thing to do with someone. I mean, not only do you get to see what they eat, but what brands and in what quantity. I wondered if the baby was going to like cream of potato soup as much as Sarah apparently did given the numerous cans she threw in her cart.

As we waited in line to pay for our groceries, Sarah made conversation with the people behind us along with the cashier. I watched her fondly. I loved how social and friendly she was. She could talk to anyone about anything. She reminded me of my dad or Danny, who both built successful sales careers off their big personalities. I wondered if Sarah could have too if she had had the same upper-middle-class childhood I had growing up, with doting parents, an excellent education, and every need not just met but surpassed.

While we began to load her groceries onto the belt, Sarah looked at me and said, "You know I smoke, right?"

"Smoke what?" I said, assuming she meant cigs but thinking it was best to clarify.

"Cigarettes," she said, laughing.

"Yeah," I said nonchalantly, pretending like it didn't bother me and also wondering where this was going.

"I've tried to quit, but it's not something I've been able to do," she said diplomatically and went on to politely ask the cashier for a pack of Pall Malls.

I dug my debit card of my purse and paid for everything. Sarah fought me on it. "You don't have to do that," she said, but I insisted because of course I was going to pay. She was giving us her baby (hopefully, anyway); the least I could do was buy her a hundred dollars' worth of groceries.

"I'll get the cigarettes then," she said.

"It's fine," I insisted, shaking her off with my hand.

"I don't know," she said. "I feel weird having you buy me cigarettes when I'm pregnant with your baby."

And then we both laughed nervously because she was right and it was weird. But adoption is 100 percent the same as cancer in that you need a sense of humor and sometimes laugh off what you can't control.

Danny was waiting for us outside. He loaded Sarah into the car first, followed by her groceries, as I returned the cart to the receptacle.

The Walmart was just a mile or two away from the garage apartment Sarah was renting from someone she'd found on Craigslist. She was able to afford it because of the monthly stipend she receives from the adoption agency. Sarah, and all birthmothers that our agency works with, receive money for rent, groceries, cab fare, maternity clothes, and other essentials they might need while pregnant. Had Sarah not been receiving financial assistance from the agency, it's very possible she would be homeless right now—and she's concerned she might be after the baby is born and the financial assistance ceases.

After walking Sarah into her apartment, meeting her cats, and looking at the pictures she showed us of the baby's father, Danny and I eventually pulled away from her house in silence. Given the last eight hours we'd had, you'd think we would have jumped right in to the play-by-play, dissecting every single thing that Sarah had said all day. But it was actually quite the opposite— we were exhausted, mentally and physically. So although I told Danny that I really liked her and that I really thought she would go through with it, and he agreed on both accounts, we were relatively quiet.

Another extreme feeling we were both battling was hunger. We'd been with Sarah for over eight hours, and I hadn't eaten a thing. Technically that puts me in what Danny calls the "danger zone" because allegedly I'm bitchy when I'm hungry. Allegedly.

I will say, however, that I kept it together as Danny flew by a Chick-fil-A upon us both agreeing that's where we'd eat. When he missed the second Chick-fil-A a few miles down the road, I again bit my tongue. It wasn't until his gas light came on that I lost it.

Are you fucking kidding?! Seriously?! When was the last time you got gas?! God! (Fine. I'm bitchy when I'm hungry.)

At last we found a shopping center with both a Chipotle and a Target, which was ideal because the first thing I wanted to do after inhaling a chicken burrito was shop for this baby! I mean, if there was ever a time I could justify a shopping trip, this was it. Besides, this was the moment that I and probably every woman who wants to have a baby had dreamed of! Shopping for your baby! Getting to pick out onesies, diapers, and a car seat! Was this really happening? It was surreal, but it also felt a little anticlimactic. Don't get me wrong—I was excited, but I was also sort of numb. Maybe I was just experiencing the whole New Year's Eve syndrome in that when you look forward to something you build it up in your head so much that it can't possibly compare to your expectations. Or perhaps it was because I was still not letting myself fully believe this was a done deal. Just moments ago at Chipotle I had instructed Danny that we wouldn't be taking the tags off anything we purchased with the exception of car seat . . . just in case. Or maybe it was Danny. I felt like his heart wasn't in the shopping trip, and I was annoyed about it. He was exhausted and, being the driver, he would have preferred to just get on the road and get back to Houston. Which I understand; it'd been a long-ass day, but I'd been waiting for this shopping trip for years!

It took about .2 seconds in Target for Danny and me to remember we were clueless in terms of babies and their respective supplies. Danny called his friend Waldo, and I could hear him being navigated through a diaper selection in the next aisle over. I, on the other hand, was in the bottle aisle. *Bottles*, I said to myself. *Hmmm* . . . After staring them down for minutes with no answer magically appearing, I decided to ask for help. Surely there was a mom somewhere in this section who would help me out. That's what moms do right? It's like a sisterhood or something?

About ten feet away I spotted a tall brunette in a white tank and black yoga pants. Not only was she hugely preggo but she had a toddler in her cart. *Perfect*, I thought. *She's a mom times two. I'll ask this chick—she'll help me, right?* As I approached her, however, she began to look vaguely familiar. *Wait a second*, I thought. *Is that . . . is that Indiana Adams?! Holy Shit! That's Indiana Adams!* (Indiana Adams a really well-known Austin blogger—one whose blog I love.)

I second-guessed asking this "mom" for help now that I knew that she was Indiana. We'd met before at a blogging conference, but I didn't know if she'd remember, and I was afraid the whole exchange would just be awkward. I gave up. On bottles. On Indiana. On life. Danny found me, now no longer in the baby section, but nearby in electronics.

Danny: What are you doing?

Me: Shhh!!!

Danny: What? Why?

Me: *(Whispering)* Indiana Adams is here.

Danny: Indiana Adams??? *(Super confused)* You mean Indiana Jones?

Me: WHAT?! *(Annoyed)* Yeah, Danny. Indiana Jones is here.

Danny: *(Excited and looking around)* Really?? Where??

Me: You're an idiot.

I eventually did ask Indiana to help me with the bottles. She was as sweet as I'd remembered her to be. She recommended I purchase the Dr. Brown bottles, so I threw a slew of those into my cart not knowing what was more surreal: the fact that I was going to be using these bottles next week or the fact that I was shopping with one of my favorite bloggers.

Wednesday, September 19, 2012
FORTY-EIGHT HOURS

It was about 4:00 p.m. today when Reagan from the agency called me. She said that Sarah had something she wanted to tell me and that I should call her right away. I wished that Reagan would have just told me the news right then and there, but I politely played along. I mean, it had to be good news, right? It'd be too cruel for Reagan to have me call Sarah knowing the news was going to be *Surprise! I've changed my mind! Ha-ha! Suckers!*

I felt the adrenaline kick in as I dialed Sarah's number. I knew this call was going to be big. She answered immediately.

"Hey, Megan! I'm getting induced tomorrow morning," she said pretty nonchalantly.

"WHAT?!" I exclaimed. "Who is this?"

She laughed, which was good as it bought me a second to think. I shouldn't have been surprised—I mean, I knew I'd be hopefully getting this call at any time now, but still. And it was a good sign, right? She's getting induced and calling us accordingly. She's doing everything she said she was gonna do, which means she's probably going to really give us this baby!

Sarah went on to say that she needed to be at the hospital at 5:30 a.m. and that she'd either take a cab or that we could pick her up if we wanted. I of course told her we'd scoop her up and then we hung up the phone. It was a fairly abbreviated call considering what she told me—I'm going to have a child tomorrow. Or, technically, in forty-eight hours from tomorrow. That's how long she has to change her mind once the baby is born. Forty-eight hours.

Thursday, September 20, 2012
HAPPY BIRTHDAY, BABY

We were playing poker. Sarah had brought a deck of cards in her overnight bag and we had eventually decided on Texas Hold 'Em even though I didn't know how to play. Danny, my dad (who had flown in from Florida that morning), and Sarah were teaching me as we went along. It was the perfect activity to be doing; not only could I tell my dad was becoming less nervous and tentative around Sarah, but it took her mind off her discomfort.

Just as I was starting to get the hang of the game Sarah had a really big contraction. She bucked back in pain and scrunched up her face waiting for it to pass. A nurse happened to be in room and asked the three of us to leave. As we waited right outside the door a nurse came out and motioned for Danny and I to come back in as she told us all nonchalantly, "It's time. She's gonna start pushing."

Danny and I were both terrified to be in the delivery room, but also honored. We were going to be able to tell our daughter that we saw her being born—that we were with her from her first breath. (Amazing!) But, let's get real here, we were about to watch a woman give birth. (Terrifying!)

I was surprised by how "animalistic" the whole birthing process was. It seemed the nurses took just as much time, if not more, preparing for the mess by putting plastic tarps down on the floor and around Sarah's bottom as they did caring for her. The birth itself went quickly—like super quickly. I think it was about three pushes and she was out. I was surprised by how direct and organized the doctor was. "Okay, Sarah, push for three seconds when I say go. Three . . . two . . . one . . . and stop. And now another push for five seconds. Start when I say go. Annnnnd go. Five . . . four . . . three . . . two . . . one."

I guess I pictured it to be more chaotic, but the doc organized the chaos, which I guess is his job.

I'll never forget the moment I saw the baby come out. She was blue and in some sort of sack that the doctor peeled her out of, and she began to cry. Seconds later, the doctor or the nurse, I don't remember who, motioned for me to come over to the bed to cut the cord. They handed me the scissors and I cut it. Upon my doing so they put her on Sarah's chest, and it was then that tears slowly slid down my cheeks. Not a full cry, but it was enough to make my eyes red in the pictures my dad took later with his iPhone.

One of the nurses asked what the baby's name was. Sarah, while looking at me, knowing the name Danny and I had chosen, told the nurse the baby's name was Macy Carter. (What she didn't tell them was Danny and I got the name Macy from the movie *Uncle Buck*, and the name Carter was in homage to Sean Carter, aka Jay-Z.)

For the next twenty minutes we all took turns holding the baby: me, my dad (who eventually got to return to the room), Danny, and Sarah. The nursing staff also got in on the rotation as they weighed her, gave her tests, and placed a pink and blue striped hat on her head.

Sarah and precious Macy left the delivery room at roughly the same time, though their destinations were completely different. Sarah had made arrangements to have a tubal procedure done right after the delivery that would prevent her from having future pregnancies. I squeezed her hand three times, like my mom used to do to me as a sign of encouragement, as the nurses rolled her out of the delivery room and down the hall to an operation room.

Macy, on the other hand, was headed to the nursery to do whatever it is newborn babies do in the nursery. Danny, my dad, and I all kinda hung out in the now empty room for a minute just looking at each other being like *what just happened*. We eventually walked down to the nursery to peek at Macy from the other side of the thick glass wall.

Her bassinet was labeled *Smith* for Sarah's last name. Sarah and Ron, Macy's birthfather, had actually given Macy their own name—I think the adoption agency encourages them to do this, perhaps as part of the grieving process. Sarah and Ron's name for the baby is the name that is now on her birth certificate and will be for the first six months. At six months, Danny, the baby, and I will go to court and the adoption will be considered final. This whole process is called "finalization." (Creative.) It's at finalization that we'll get a new birth certificate with the name "Macy" and Danny and I named as her parents. Just to be clear, Sarah and Ron have no legal rights concerning Macy during these six months— their rights are 100 percent forfeited after the forty-eight hours ceases (for Texas anyway, every state has different rules regarding adoption).

I looked at Macy, whose bassinet was placed directly next to that of a huge, ten-pound Asian baby—a sumo-wrestler-looking thing. Macy, being only five pounds, four ounces, looked like a peanut next to him. A tiny, cute, precious peanut. My peanut . . . in forty-eight hours . . . hopefully.

Friday, September 21, 2012
SLUMBER PARTY

Danny and I were supposed to have our own room last night. This hospital we're at usually gives adoptive parents their own room so they have somewhere to go during their forty-eight-hour wait. The hospital is so packed this weekend, though, that they didn't have a room to give us. I wasn't too disappointed finding this out. I was exhausted and knew a good night of sleep was in store for me if we made the forty-five-minute drive back to Danny's mom's house, since she conveniently lived in Austin. Not to mention, Booker was there!

When Sarah asked me to spend the night with her, however, I couldn't say no. Not only because I was deathly afraid to do anything to upset her—afraid it'd provoke her to change her mind—but I also felt bad for her and wanted support her. With the exception of Ron and a girlfriend she'd talked to on the phone a few times, no one in Sarah's life knew about her pregnancy. Not her mom, not her stepdad, not her sisters, not Ron's family. She kept the secret by keeping her distance from her family during the pregnancy and wearing baggy stuff when she did. If Sarah wanted me to spend the night with her, I wasn't going to leave the poor girl alone. You'd have to be coldhearted to do such a thing.

Danny and my dad went to retrieve my suitcase from the car after I told them I'd be staying with Sarah. By the time they brought it back up to me I was already laying down on the window ledge that doubled as a guest bed in Sarah's room. Danny kissed me good-bye, and I gave him my donut order for the morning (chocolate Long John, obvi, and a few donut holes for good measure).

Saying I was exhausted is the understatement of the world. Sarah, however, despite giving birth that day, showed no signs of slowing down. She was a night owl to begin with and had told me that she intended to stay awake the full forty-eight hours we were in the hospital as she didn't want to waste any of her precious time with the baby, who she was holding in her lap. "I can sleep when I go home," she told me.

As I pinched myself in an effort to stay awake, Sarah talked my ear off about everything under the sun. I got more information about her other kids, Macy's half-siblings. They were from Sarah's first marriage—a marriage Sarah dropped out of high school sophomore year to make.

Sarah told me about a short stint in rehab for alcohol. She was roommates with a HUGE celebrity's sister, and I hung on her every word as she told me not just about the sister, but the celebrity as well, as this A-lister would visit often. Sarah was a great storyteller and she was telling stories about my favorite subject: celebrities. This was awesome!

Sarah told me how she met Ron six years ago at Bennigan's. He was a line cook and she was a hostess until she was promoted to be a waitress and eventually the manager. I could picture Sarah being the manager, with her great people skills and affinity for rules. She was constantly telling me about "the rules"—the rules at this hospital, the rules at the adoption agency, and the rules at rehab. Sarah seemed to like boundaries and knowing what she was allowed and *not* allowed to do.

I asked Sarah if she learned to cook at Bennigan's. She told me that though her expertise in basting an egg came from her years there, the majority of her cooking knowledge came from her grandma.

I loved learning more about Sarah, and the more information I got, the more I was able to piece together how this twenty-seven-year-old girl had arrived at exactly where she was in this moment.

As Sarah and I chatted, I was conscious of how important this moment—right there, right then—was. I have every intention of Sarah being in our life forever, but if, God forbid, something tragic should happen, these stories would be all I'd have to share with Macy about her birthmother. Sarah seemed strong right now, but the truth is, not a lot was going her way. She was a recovering addict (though had been clean throughout this pregnancy) and soon she wasn't going to have any source of income or a place to live. The odds, realistically, were stacked against her. I genuinely didn't see Sarah going off the grid, but I knew there were no guarantees. I needed to internalize every word she was saying, not for me, but for Macy. But with each sentence Sarah strung together, my eyelids became heavier and heavier. I eventually surrendered to sleep.

I continued to drift in and out of deep REM cycles, each time waking to find Sarah still wide awake. Once I opened my eyes just long enough to see her walking out of the bathroom, apparently just having showered, with a towel turban on her head. Hours later I rolled over to see her writing furiously in her spiral notebook. At 5:00 a.m. I woke up to the creak of the door and saw a nurse popping her head in to check on Macy. The nurses had been doing that since we'd been there, making sure Macy was eating enough, peeing in her diaper, etc.

The nurse's face changed, however, as soon as she saw Sarah was feeding the baby. They exchanged quick words, and I tried to piece together what was happening. Something about Sarah feeding the baby with formula that had been sitting out too long maybe? Sarah said she didn't do it, but this nurse was visibly angry.

Had it been up to me, Macy wouldn't have even been in the room with us. I would have preferred her to be in the nursery so I'd know she was getting the best care—plus it would have allowed Sarah and me to sleep. But because Sarah had a mere forty-eight hours to spend with the baby (her baby, let's not forget), I could completely understand that she wanted to make the most of the time, so I'd bit my tongue.

I felt like this whole formula situation was my fault. It *was* my fault. It was the first time I had needed to protect my baby, and I had failed because I was "tired." Pathetic. I told Sarah that I had to go to the bathroom and ran out the door to find the nurse. Before I could even form any words to speak to her, I was crying. I could feel her judging me, in my Jay-Z sweatshirt, black sweatpants, and zilch makeup—I looked seventeen at best. I could tell she thought I must have been a teenage friend of Sarah's.

I felt like I had to explain myself. "I'm the adoptive mom," I stammered. "I fell asleep . . . what's happening . . . is the baby going to be okay?" I asked, tears now more prevalent.

Her face immediately softened. "Oh, honey. Yeah. She'll be fine. Just keep an eye on her in there." And then she went on to say, "I'm glad the baby is going home with you."

And that pissed me off. I mean, I was glad the baby was going home with me too; I hoped she was, anyway. But she didn't need to say that. It was then I realized Sarah was family. I mean, I'd known that Sarah was "family" in that, for the rest of our lives, we were both going to be able to call this baby our daughter. But she was becoming family in a way that I was much more familiar with—in that *I* am the only person allowed to talk shit about my family. If anyone else does it, I'll fight them. Stupid-ass nurse.

I wiped the tears off my face and looked at my phone. It was almost 6:00 a.m. I stopped at the floor's coffee machine and poured myself the world's nastiest cup of coffee. (Seriously, so gross.) I then shot off a rather urgent text to Danny and my dad to get to the hospital ASAP.

Saturday, September 22, 2012
I LOVE YOU, MACY

Today started around 6:00 a.m. when I once again awoke at Sarah's bedside. Danny was originally going to stay the night with her. Not just because I wanted a night off from the hospital scene, but because Sarah and I had bonded so much last night. I wanted Danny to have the opportunity to do so as well. At the very last minute, though, I could tell he really didn't want to, and I wasn't going to make him. Plus it was probably weirder for him to do so, being male and all.

Sarah had a rough night. Being up for a straight thirty-six hours was beginning to take its toll and she was becoming a little unglued. She was irritable when the nurses wouldn't give her her preferred dosage of pain medicine, she was crying a lot, and just overall exhausted. Thankfully we had a really bossy young nurse who basically forced a sleeping pill down Sarah's throat. It eventually made her fall asleep, which meant I got to sleep worry-free as the baby was in the nursery.

Reagan came up to the hospital in the morning to meet with Sarah and do a little counseling to get ready for the paperwork she'd sign later that afternoon, a standard procedure on the agency's part. After their session, Reagan told us she was going into her office to get some work done and she'd be back in a few hours to do the deal. Danny, my dad, and I all chilled in Sarah's room, tooling around our computers, watching the news, and overall just waiting for the clock to get there. Sarah took frequent smoke breaks when she'd usually want me to accompany her. After one of them we took a trip to the hospital gift shop, where I could tell she wanted to buy the baby a gift. I watched her as she checked the price tag on everything she touched. She eventually found a onesie that said *Worth the Wait* on it. It was eight dollars, but for Sarah that could have been the last few dollars to her name, another generous gesture on her part.

I couldn't have been happier to see anyone in the world when Reagan reappeared at 3:00 p.m. to start Sarah's paperwork. Danny, my dad, and I quickly left the crowded room to let the two of them begin. I didn't know the specifics of what was going to go down, but this was adoption—if one thing was certain, there was going to be a shitload of paperwork.

About an hour later Reagan came and found Danny and me in the waiting room. She pulled up a seat and assured us Sarah had signed and was doing "as well as was to be expected" under the circumstances. Now it was our turn. Danny stood up and grabbed a small table from the other side of the room and placed it in front of us. We then began to sign our lives away. Reagan had to read all sixty-seven pages aloud to us, and it was painful. Not because Reagan is a bad reader or has an unpleasant voice— it just made the process that much longer and I was anxious to be done.

Somehow, we eventually were finished. We all stood up, including my dad, who was just a seat or two away when we were signing the paperwork. We gathered our things and started the thirty-second walk back to Sarah's hospital room, where she was waiting for us to come get Macy. The sense of dread and heartbreak got more and more suffocating the closer we inched to the door. I was already sobbing in anticipation of the moment, and my dad, though I'm sure he doesn't appreciate me saying so, was crying as well.

We all pulled the Band-Aid off quickly. My dad cried and Sarah sobbed as they hugged, and I overheard him whisper, *Take care of yourself, Sweetie,* in her ear. Then Danny hugged her and I suppose I was next. To be honest, I don't really remember even though it was just hours ago. All I remember is sobbing so hard that I couldn't catch my breath, telling Sarah I loved her, and hearing her cry just as hard. It was a moment that made even my darkest cancer days seem frivolous and silly.

Danny and my Dad exited the room first as I trailed behind them. Sarah remained on bed sobbing. I assume Reagan was still there to console her. I don't know for certain. There was no way I could stomach looking back over my shoulder to see for sure. As I took my final step through the doorway, pushing and navigating Macy's bassinet in the process, Sarah half yelled/half moaned, *I LOVE YOU, MACY*, just as the door slammed behind me. It's a moment that will haunt me for the rest of my life.

Friday, September 28, 2012
E-MAIL CORRESPONDENCE

To: megan@hotmail.com; danny@hotmail.com
From: sarah8910@gmail.com
Subject: Megan & Danny

Megan and Danny, thank you. For loving her and giving her what she deserves. Y'all are a gift from God sent for that angel. I know everything that I chose to do was the right decision. She is very blessed to have y'all as her parents. And I am very blessed as well to have you as friends. Thank you for not pushing me away. For allowing me to be a part of her life, I am eternally grateful. I love y'all very much.

To: sarah8910@gmail.com
From: megan@hotmail.com; danny@hotmail.com
Subject: RE: Megan & Danny

Sarah,

I always thought the day Danny and I came home from the hospital with a baby, biological or adopted alike, it would be the best day of our life. I know now that isn't true. Don't get me wrong. I love Macy with everything I have, but I can't fully enjoy her presence because my heart is breaking for you. Please know that there isn't a minute that has gone by since I've been home that I'm not thinking of you, grieving for you, and hoping you're okay. How can I be happy for me when I'm so sad for you?

I know it will get easier for both of us. Time heals everything but it doesn't erase it. I will NEVER be able to repay you for the gift you gave us. What I can do, however, is take care of that little girl—our little girl—like no little girl has been cared for before. I can take care of her so she never needs or wants for anything. (Well, she can want for some stuff . . . we don't want her being a spoiled diva!) That little girl will be the most loved girl in the entire planet. Between me and Danny, you and Ron, and both our subsequent families, that are now forever joined, she is the luckiest little girl in the whole entire world. All because of you.

I love you so much. Thank you.

~Megan

Tuesday, January 8, 2013
EPILOGUE

MD Anderson is full of good energy. Every time I leave there, I'm inspired by it. My most recent trip was no different. It was a week before Christmas, and the place was decked out with trees, wreaths, and red bows galore. There were even carolers singing right outside the diagnostic lab where I was waiting to get blood drawn. I was sitting on the very outskirts of the lab, partly so I could hear the music and partly so I could keep Danny and Macy within sight. They couldn't sit with me, as children under twelve aren't allowed to be in the lab, which I think Danny was excited about, as it meant he got to sit front row to the carolers.

I watched him show off Macy to the random people that came up to him, as I've learned people do when you have a baby. I never mind it, especially here, where to me Macy is just as much a part of our community as any other patient. You see, Macy is, as far as I'm concerned, the ending to my cancer story. Macy is what I, along with the help of Dr. Bear, Dr. Alex, and even the doctors in Chicago and Boston, worked so hard to protect. And even though we didn't necessarily preserve my fertility in the end, it doesn't even matter, because I have Macy, who is just as perfect, if not more, than any baby Danny and I could make.

Macy is almost four months old now. Part of me can't believe it, feeling like it was just yesterday I was in that hospital room with Sarah, watching her try to con more pain medicine out of the nurse than they wanted to give her. (Ha! Who does that sound like?) But the other part of me feels like Macy has been with us for years.

I loved Macy right away—even while she was still in Sarah's stomach. Feeling like her mom, however, didn't come as quick.

I don't know if that's an adoption thing, a five-day-turnaround adoption thing, or maybe biological parents feel this way too? Regardless, it's just recently that I'm starting to feel "that bond" or that I'm Macy's mom—not Macy's caretaker. Maybe it's because she's old enough now that I can tickle her and kiss her neck all while she giggles and squeals in delight. It's amazing, and I feel like her mom when I do it.

We've seen Sarah twice now in just the four months that Macy's been alive. The first time was at Thanksgiving. We were spending in Austin at Danny's mom's place anyway, so it was convenient for us to arrange to meet Sarah at the agency. Now unable to afford her garage apartment, Sarah had moved in with her mom and stepdad. More so than that, she had ended up telling her mom about Macy and the adoption. Her mom thankfully was very supportive and told Sarah it was the best decision that she'd ever made. Sarah's stepdad told her he was proud of her, which I could tell meant so much to her.

Danny and I brought Sarah and her mom calla lilies when we met them at the agency. We met in the same room we had been in the very first time we met Sarah, when she was still pregnant and I had felt the baby kick. This meeting was just as emotional as the last one, but this time more so for Sarah and her mom.

Seeing Macy for the first time since the hospital was going to be emotional for Sarah regardless, but having her mom with her, showing her mom the beautiful thing that she'd made and done meant it was that much more emotional. I can only imagine what an enormous weight she felt lifted off her shoulders.

There were times during the visit that Sarah sobbed so hard she couldn't catch her breath. Danny and I stepped out of the room a few times to try to give Sarah, her mom, and the baby some private moments. It wasn't all heavy though; we shared some laughs as well.

As it always does, Christmas came just a month later, and Danny and I were again spending it in Austin. Having just seen Sarah last month, we wouldn't have met up with her again so soon, but learned that if we did, we'd have the opportunity to meet Ron.

Because Danny had to work late, we arranged to meet up on a Friday night. Because the adoption agency wouldn't be open then, I suggested we meet for pizza. Not knowing Austin terribly well, I asked my friends who lived there what a good pizza place would be for the occasion. They recommended Frank and Angie's, which was perfect—not pretentious at all, just a little a hole in the wall if anything. I think all four of us felt comfortable there, or as comfortable as you can be given the situation.

Ron was exactly what I expected him to be. Nice guy, warm, easy to talk to. He thanked Danny and me several times throughout the meal for doing "what we did," which was obviously unnecessary. If anything, we should have been thanking him.

I took a bunch of pictures at the pizza place: Sarah and Ron, Ron and the baby, Sarah and the baby, all three of them together, and we even got our waitress to take a few of the five of us. I've since mailed the pictures to Sarah, and technically Ron too as he's temporarily living at Sarah's mom's house. I bet it's safe to say, however, they don't need copies of those pictures. I think they'll remember that night in their minds for the rest of their lives just as vividly as I will—not that anything crazy happened. It was just the first time the five of us were together and that in itself makes it special. No matter how you slice it (Slice it! Pizza! Ha!), the four of us are Macy's parents.

For the rest of her life, Macy will have four parents. That's gonna be hard sometimes. But it is what it is. We wouldn't have precious Macy without Sarah and Ron, so to not acknowledge, respect, and love them accordingly isn't an option for us. It'd be living a lie.

I don't know when we'll see Sarah and Ron again. We hear weekly from Sarah via text, usually on Sundays during football. She likes to check in on the Bears. It's up to every adoptive parent/birthparent unit to decide what works for them. I know Danny and I'd love to see Ron and Sarah twice a year—maybe once in the summer and once around Christmas time. Not always just meals either, but working up to fun outings like bowling or something as Macy gets older. We'll just have to take it a day at a time. But it's definitely important to us that Macy knows who they are, so that she can feel whole, and have closure, never wondering where she came from or what her birthparents were like.

Recently one of my dad's friends, a spunky, vivacious woman who I'm guessing is in her late sixties, came up to me at a party and was very interested in the details of Macy's adoption. I had no idea why she was so interested or why this woman I'd just met was becoming so emotional. It turned out that she herself was adopted, and she told me that every day she thought about her birthmother. She was born during "the war" and guessed that perhaps her birthmother had gotten up knocked up while her husband was overseas—but of course that was just a guess. And even though this woman grew up in a great home, with loving parents, she still wondered. Every day, for sixty-something years. That is the opposite of what I want for Macy. I want to put it all out there for her, so she can come to learn, know, and love Sarah and Ron just as much for their faults as their strengths, as Danny and I do.

Upon finishing my blood test, I walked out of the lab and spotted Danny and a slew of people crowded around something I could only assume was Macy. I approached the crowd, smiled at all the people, most of them elderly patients or their spouses, and then Danny and I headed to the hospital café for a quick lunch before my appointment with Dr. Alex.

Danny got Macy and me settled at a table and then went to grab us sandwiches. As I was sitting there, messing with Macy, I realized my arm was still bleeding, so much so that it had bled through my Band-Aid and was about to get on my shirt. Just as I was about to pick Macy up so I could grab some napkins, the lady eating next to me got up, dropped a handful of Band-Aids down on my table, sat back down, and continued eating her pasta. *Thanks*, I mouthed at her. She smiled back at me but with a look that said, *Oh please, are you seriously thanking me for a Band-Aid?* I love MD Anderson.

The gynecologic oncology floor is on six. I pushed the elevator button accordingly and thought about how I'd just recently learned how to pronounce *Gynecologic Oncology*. For years it sounded like I was having a stroke when attempting to say it. I checked in at the front desk while Danny and Macy set up shop in the waiting room. Once again, from afar, I spotted Danny talking to a family, all peering in at Macy in her car seat.

The nurse eventually called my name, and Danny and I found ourselves in the examination room as we had so many times before. I had actually just been here three weeks prior. I was returning today only to re-take my CA-125 blood test as the results three weeks ago were "elevated."

We didn't have to sweat it out long. Dr. Alex's nurse practitioner came in and told us my results this time had gone back down. I was all good.

"Really?" I asked happily. "Then do you think we can go? Danny is playing Santa at his company's Christmas party, and if we don't leave now he's not going to make it."

She laughed. "Let me go grab Dr. Alex and make sure she doesn't want to examine you."

Dr. Alex came in and cooed at Macy. "You can go," she said while still looking at the baby. "I don't need to examine you."

Now focusing on me, she said, "I'll just schedule you to come back in two months. Sound good?"

"Yeah," I said. "That sounds good."

"Do you have any questions?" she asked.

"Nope," I said, smiling.

She smiled back at me as though we had an inside joke. There was no joke, though. I was just happy and in a good mood and she could tell.

"All right. Well, I want to see pictures of Danny as Santa," she told us, still smiling as she walked out.

I quickly changed out of my gown and put on my clothes as Danny swung Macy's diaper bag over his shoulder. He had less than an hour to make it to his office, and he had to drop the baby and me off at home first. We were practically running down the hallway back to the waiting room when a nurse I'd never seen before stopped us.

"Is that your baby?" she asked quizzically as she looked me up and down.

"Yeah," I said as I opened the door to exit, waiting to see if she was going to say anything else.

"Huh," she said. "Well, you sure did get your figure back fast."

"Thanks," I said as I shut the door. And then I started laughing. And so did Danny. And so did Macy.

ACKNOWLEDGEMENTS

Being an author when I grew up was never the plan. My mom claims I wanted to be "a waitress" when I was little. (What she doesn't know is that I meant at Hooters.) This book, however, is just one of the many wonderful things that came into my life because of cancer. Cancer is a weird thing to be grateful for, but I am—it changed my life for the better. Speaking of grateful, I have some people I'd like to thank.

Thank you to Brown Books Publishing Group.

Thank you to my unofficial editors: Ron Haney, Lydia Criss Mays, and my mom.

Paige Budde: thanks, *girrrrrrl*, for my author photo.

Thank you to my immediate family: my mom, my dad, my brother, and Julianna.

Thank you to everyone at MD Anderson—especially "Dr. Alex." My life would still be very different today had I not come to MDA for a third opinion. It's a special place, and I'm proud to be part of its community, even if it's just as a patient. Dr. Alex, I'm pretty sure you had no idea I was writing this book, so I hope you're not super creeped out. Thank you for being a super smart and legit doctor. I'm able to be so nonchalant about my cancer because I know I'll always be okay under your watch.

Thank you to Macy's birthmother and father. We think about you every day and love you.

Last and certainly not least, thank you to Danny. I don't know which was harder: living this story or the process of writing and publishing it. Either way, they're both things I couldn't have done without you. You're my constant source of encouragement, support, confidence, and happiness. I love you.

ABOUT THE AUTHOR

Megan Silianoff is a writer best known for her popular blog *Greetings From Texas*. She resides in Houston, though if this book does well enough she'd love to move to Malibu. Visit Megan's blog at www.GreetingsFromTX.com and find her on Twitter @GreetingsFromTX.